LOYALL W

THE
KING
OF NO:
A FINANCIAL
FIREFIGHTER

Loyall Wilson

Table of Contents

CHAPTER 1

The Right Fit at the Right Time

I WORKED FOR one of the largest investment firms in the country. My official title was Executive Vice President and Chief Compliance Officer. While I also held several other titles, such as Chief Anti-Money Laundering Officer, Chief Cyber Security Officer, and President of one of our smaller subsidiary broker-dealers, my best-known titles were the ones people whispered behind my back, like Mr. Compliance, Vice President of the Sales Prevention Team.

Or, you know, the one you shouldn't say in any sales organization: the "N" word—no, not that "N" word. The other one. The one that no salesperson ever wants to hear: "no." As a matter of fact, they called me the "King of No."

Like many sales organizations, one of their top goals was getting to "yes." Getting the clients to say "yes," getting the home office to say "yes," and getting compliance to say "yes."

But as my mom used to say, "Too much of a good thing isn't good for you, and you can't always have your way." Someone had to say "no," and that someone was me.

When I took this job, I had no idea what I was in for, that I would become the first and only African American officer in the history of the company and, by the end of my career, I would have fired a few dozen people and put a few dozen more in prison for stealing millions of dollars from clients.

This was a very good company, and I made the right choice joining it. Although I wasn't sure at first. I didn't really need a new job; I was quite comfortable with the one I had. But there was no harm in looking. The company was well respected in the industry, although a little too conservative for me. But being conservative gives you strength and longevity, and the parent company was 130 years old. Still, it was much smaller than other companies I had worked for, such as Merrill Lynch, Charles Schwab, and Olde Stock Brokers.

My phone interview with the vice president of human resources was a piece of cake. Setting up a meeting with the president of the company, proved more challenging, though. He was a busy man, traveling all over the country. Eventually, we found that we were both going to be at an NASD (National Association of Securities Dealers) conference in Washington, DC, so we met there for lunch.

You can tell when someone is trying to hide a look of surprise. The caption I saw over his head was an unmistakable one I'd seen many times before: "Oh my God, he's black." He recovered quickly, though, and we had a nice lunch. I went on talking about my experience and what I'd accomplished in my career. All he talked about was how cold it was in Minnesota and how did I feel about winter?

I assume that part of the interview went well too, because he invited me back to the home office in Minnesota. Then the interview process took a nosedive. It started with the psychological evaluation, which I think I failed.

The written part was no problem, it was the face-to-face meeting with the shrink, Dr. Korvac, that was problematic. Apparently, the company had its own psychologist on staff. I felt uncomfortable the moment I stepped into his office. He asked questions about my life that had nothing to do with my resume or my qualifications.

"What were your hobbies in high school?"

"High school?" I said. "That was thirty-five years ago."

"You grew up in an interesting time, in an interesting city. What was that like?"

I'm sure he was talking about the riots in Detroit in the sixties. I told him I didn't see where that was any concern of his. "You should keep your questions to the information on my resume and my quali-fications," I said.

I could see from his expression he had no one speak to him that way before.

He said it was important for him to get to know me to see if I was a good fit for the company. He saw I was in the Navy during the Vietnam War and he asked, "What was that experience like?" and "How were you able to deal with that?"

I told him, "God. God is how I deal with the vast majority of things in my life. Do you have any more questions about my work experience?"

He said, "I'm just trying to get to know you."

"I didn't tell my friends about it, so there's no way I'm going to share that experience with you."

"This is a normal part of the interview process for someone at this level."

"I worked on the floor of the Pacific Stock Exchange, Merrill Lynch, and Charles Schwab," I told him. "I worked on the line at Ford Motor Company for six years, and I had an honorable discharge from the U.S. Navy. I've never been in jail. I never did drugs, and I've never been in trouble." That was true except for one little incident aboard ship when I was in the Navy. Some drunk asshole wondered what it would be like to piss on a black guy while he was sleeping in the bottom bunk. The problem for him was that I was a light sleeper. Afterward, they airlifted him to a hospital and threw me in the brig for the day. He never came back, and I moved to a top bunk.

Other than that, I've been good. But anyway, my personal life was mine, and as long as it didn't have a negative impact on my work, it was none of his business.

Dr. Korvac said, "I don't think you understand the importance of this part of the interview process. It's important that I get to know you, but I feel you're being uncooperative."

"Look, Dr. Korvac, I would be happy to cooperate on any ques-tions regarding my qualifications and work history. But if you think

I'm going to share my innermost feelings just because you asked me, well, that's not going to happen. I know I'm well qualified for the job, so you'll have to make your recommendations based on the information you have. It was a pleasure to meet you but I need to prepare for my next interview."

With that, I shook his hand and left.

I guess some of my answers would have been different if I needed the job. But I didn't. I wasn't sure if he had ever interviewed an African American before, or maybe he was just collecting information for a book. I didn't really know, but I would not be one of his subjects. Later, I heard that he said I was very smart and knowledgeable about compliance and the industry as a whole, but somewhat uncooperative.

Not that I had anything to hide about my past. I think Dr. Korvac and I had different goals for that part of the interview process. He wanted to go beyond my qualifications. He wanted to make sure I could be a good Stepford Wife and be easily assimilated into their culture; for him, it was just same drill, different day.

The problem, and I think the president of the firm knew this, was the company needed a change master. Someone who wasn't cut from the same cookie-cutter pattern they'd been hiring from for years. Sometimes you have to shake things up, and what they needed was a tough kid from the Eastside of Detroit, with that unusual combination of street smarts, book smarts, and military toughness. Someone strong enough to stand his ground in a fight but smart enough to know when to negotiate instead of fighting.

Someone who wasn't afraid to work hard, and who had the background in the industry to gain the respect of the field force.

The president decided to take a chance on me, so I took a chance on him.

It's not every day you get to work for someone as smart, fearless and as strong as he was. You have to respect a man willing to have the "black factor" conversation (I made the term up, but it works). But the conversation went like this: "Based on the history and make-up of this company, you being black will probably play a role in how far you can move up in this company. I just don't know how much of a role it will play. But I can promise you this, if you stick with me, I will back you every step of the way. It may take a while, but together we will make a difference."

Most people know the black factor exists but wouldn't dare bring it up in the interview process. My respect level for him doubled when he had the courage and honesty to give me full disclosure right up front.

And for that, I gave him my best. I'm not sure I was ever a *good* fit, but I was the *right* fit at the *right* time.

CHAPTER 2

The Transformation

YOU MIGHT WONDER, like Dr. Korvac did, how I went from six years as a robot on the line in a Ford Motor Company factory to the floor of the Pacific Stock Exchange. I know my cousin Mike, back in Detroit, used to run around asking people, "Why is Loyall lying about his job in California?"

The fact is, I wasn't lying. I never wanted to work in the factory. But when I came home from the service, they were just throwing those jobs at veterans.

I tried going to night school to get my bachelor's degree, but it was tough after working twelve-hour shifts. One time, I fell asleep in class and the teacher turned the lights off and left me there. The next night, I pinned his ass against the wall and cussed him out. "I know you think I'm some kind of fucking junkie, but I'm not! I work twelve hours a day on the line and then come to class at night. I'm sorry I fell asleep in your class, but if you ever turn the lights out on me and leave me there again, I will put my foot in your ass."

I think some of the other people in the class understood what I was going through, so they would kick my chair every now and then to make sure I was awake.

I knew God had other plans for me, and I soon found out what they were. One winter, while I was driving home in the snow after one of those twelve-hour shifts, I looked in the rearview mirror and saw that God had guided my car out of the ditch and back onto the highway. I had fallen asleep, and God had kicked my chair to wake me up.

I went home and made plans to move to Los Angeles. I don't know why I chose L.A. There are a lot of places that don't have snow. But it sounded good rolling off my lips. My cousin Bun told me that if I let his friend, Leon ride with me to Los Angeles, he could get me a job on the floor of the PSE—the Pacific Stock Exchange. I didn't know what it was, but it was a job, so I said, "Ok, let's go."

There I was, in the glamour capital of the world. Mountains, beaches, beautiful women, and no snow. Only two weeks after arriving, I ran into my first movie star, and I didn't even know it. I was playing a little one-on-one basketball with a close friend, Gee, when this guy walked up with a woman on his arm. She was finer than daylight, so I barely noticed him.

He asked if he could play a game with us, and we said sure, why not? After introductions, we had a friendly game of twenty-one. He wasn't much of a player. I think he was just showing off in front of his woman. And I didn't blame him. He was a little wild, though, and I got tired of him hacking me, so I strong-armed him a couple of times. I hurt nothing but his pride. After the game, he thanked us and started off on his way.

As he was walking away I heard Gee ask him, "How was that *Romancing the Stone*?"

He said, "Great, you should go see it!"

I asked Gee, "What the hell are you talking about, 'romancing the stone'?"

He said, "The movie."

"Why would you ask him about a movie?"

"Don't you know who that was?"

"Should I?"

"That was Michael Douglas."

"The actor? And you let me knock him down?"

"Ah, fool. He wanted a real game. You gave it to him, and he enjoyed it."

The time came for my interview at the PSE. It was really my first interview, and I didn't know what to expect. At my last job, you just filled out an application and waited for a call saying you were hired.

The manager on the floor introduced himself and asked if I was Leon's friend. I said yes, and he said, "Ok, you can start on Monday."

God is so good.

The next thing I knew, I was a runner on the floor of the PSE, wearing a white shirt and tie I borrowed from Leon. All I knew was that I didn't smell like oil. (It took a week of scrubbing to finally get all the factory grunge out from under my fingernails!) From the floor of a factory to the floor of the exchange … what a difference a day makes.

I had no idea where I was or how much money was flowing through that place. The specialists were making so much money that one day, when the exchange caught fire, they refused to leave their seats or stop trading. Smoke was filling up the place, and the firefighters had to put out the blaze around them.

In those days, the PSE in Los Angeles was a dually connected floor with the PSE in San Francisco. One day, the clerks in L.A. played a game of basketball with the clerks in San Francisco. The specialists got together and flew the San Francisco clerks down; instead of getting a gym at a local high school or something, they rented the Forum where the Los Angeles Lakers played. That's how much money they had. Our feet were about to touch the same floor as the Lakers. So, of course, we all had to buy new shoes.

There were times I thought God missed my chair and kicked me in the head because I had a headache every day. But that was from having to think for the first time in six years. You do little thinking on the line: put a screw in here, tighten a bolt there. Now I had to learn the symbols for all the stocks traded on the floor—and for that matter, learn how the stock market worked. I had to listen to specialists bellow out orders, keep track of them, and make sure they were delivered in good order to be posted on the ticker tape. I was knee-deep in the quicksand of the financial markets, and I was sinking fast.

For some reason, one of the specialists took me under his wing. He told me about the library up on the thirtieth floor and which books I should read.

He also advised me to cut my Michael Jackson-sized afro—you know, the one he had before the transformation.

I was like, "What? Are you serious?"

He said, "Look, I'm going to be honest with you. This is a white man's world. Look around you. They look at you, with your big afro hair, and they think *militant*. I'd like to see you succeed, and I think this small adjustment would go a long way to increasing your acceptance around here and turning their short-sided negative perception into a positive one."

I got a little angry at first. But then I thought maybe God was using someone else to kick my chair. Sometimes you have to take two steps back to take one step forward. So, I cut my hair. It's been short every day of my life since.

I studied day and night until I got my Series 7—the stockbroker license. Over the next few years, I got about a dozen more licenses and certifications. Turns out that once I started thinking again, I was pretty good at it.

But the Series 7 was special. That was the license that decided where you would go in this business. It was the key to a lot of locked doors. It was so big that a bunch of my friends took me to a ritzy restaurant in Hollywood to celebrate.

We were in a large booth with those high-back Victorian seats, so we could see no one beside us. Suddenly (I guess we were making a lot of noise), a woman in the next booth stood up on her seat and asked us what all the commotion was about. I didn't have to ask who she was. It was Dolly Parton, the famous country singer and actress.

We were all shocked, but she must have talked with us for about a half an hour. Then when we went to cash out, would you believe she paid our entire bill and sent us two bottles of champagne? What a wonderful blessing. Thank you, Miss Parton.

I was like a sponge, learning everything I could. Leon and I saved our money up to get a "two-dollar booth" on the floor of the exchange.

Those are on the side of the floor for brokers to trade their own stocks at no commission. But sometimes, when the specialist needed help, the two-dollar brokers would get to trade some leftover stocks too.

Merrill Lynch had just moved part of their back-office operation from New York to Los Angeles, and they were paying more than the PSE. So, I quickly got a job there and learned the stock-brokerage business. Leon liked the limelight and running with the big dogs, but I was more of the quiet bookworm type. So he stayed on the floor and I worked for Merrill Lynch's operation center. Dreams have a way of not always working out the way you want. That limelight and drugs got the best of Leon, and God was about to kick my chair again.

It wasn't until I worked for Merrill Lynch in Beverly Hills that I got into compliance. I was walking down Rodeo Drive during lunch— I couldn't afford lunch, so I walked a lot—when I saw an elderly woman driving the wrong way down the one-way street. I joked, "She looks like one of Neil's clients."

Neil was one of the top brokers in the Beverly Hills office. Lo and behold, when I got back, that lady was sitting in his office. Neil had just sold her a million-dollar thoroughbred racehorse limited partnership. People were patting him on the back, congratulating him, and teasing him about how much money he would make on it. All I could think about was, "If that was my grandmother, I'd put my foot in Neil's behind." It was a totally unsuitable investment for her.

A Moment …

In those days, suitability wasn't a requirement as long as the client understood the risk. For some brokers, if the check cleared then it was suitable. I was not one of those people. Ask yourself whether a particular product is right for you. Don't just ask if it pays a higher dividend or more interest. There's a lot of truth in the old saying, the higher the return, the higher the risk. So, ask yourself, "Can I afford the risk? Can I afford to lose this money?" Then decide.

The very next day, the office manager told me she got a memo from corporate in New York saying she had to hire a compliance officer. I asked her what a compliance officer was. She told me that compliance is like internal affairs at the police department. Compliance officers are responsible for enforcing the rules and regulations set by the company itself, the states, the SEC (Security Exchange Commission) and the NASD (National Association of Security Dealers, now known as FINRA, the Financial Industry Regulatory Authority).

"A compliance officer's job is like the Maytag repairman," she told me. "It's a very lonely job. No one really likes them because they're always saying no to stockbrokers and telling people what they can't do. But compliance is one of the most important departments in the company. Compliance is the gatekeeper, and I would say the heart and soul of a company. The job of a compliance officer is to protect the client, the firm, and the stockbroker from themselves."

Compliance was becoming the new buzzword in the industry, following the news about Michael Milken and others selling "junk bonds." That's when God kicked my chair again to wake me up. I always knew my calling in life was to protect people. As a compliance officer, I could make a difference. I could stop people like Neil from taking advantage of unknowing elderly people.

So I told her, "I would love to be a compliance officer."

CHAPTER 3

The Blank Check

THE FIRST REAL case I was involved in was a $5,000,000 inside job involving one registered rep and two home-office people. While you may find this hard to believe, sometimes clients were very lax when it came to properly filling out a check they sent to Merrill Lynch. Sometimes, the checks were made out to Merrill, to Smith, to ML, and, to my surprise, some would just leave it blank. We discovered that a stockbroker in the Los Angeles office was opening accounts in fictitious names and splitting the money with his partners in the home office.

If a client sent a check in with the payee line blank, this person would take the check and write the name of one of their partners in the payee line. If the check just had the initials ML on it, they might open an account in the name of ML Smith or M. Larson, for example, then the broker would open an account in the fictitious name, and have someone pull the money out. The real client might not find out until thirty days later when they got their statements—assuming they read them at all.

Compliance officers are always looking for "red flags" or tips. The first red flag in this case was the home-office person arriving at work in a brand-new Mercedes-Benz he bragged about paying cash for (when he was only making $20,000 a year). We took a while to con-nect all the dots, but I felt a great deal of pride and satisfaction when I came to work one day and the FBI were leading the broker and the home-office person away in handcuffs. For the first time in my life, I had a job that gave me a sense of purpose. Something that fulfilled my need to protect people.

Where did this need come from? I wanted to be a fireman when I was young, but I failed the physical—I was too short. Don't laugh! The requirements were different back then.

I joined the Navy to "see the world" and to protect my country. I would fight anyone to protect my brother and sister when I was young. I even lied for them when they did something wrong, to protect them, so that my mother would whip me instead of them.

I wanted to protect little kids from bullies in the neighborhood too. I once got jumped by a gang of boys in front of my parents' house. Instead of running inside and possibly putting them in the line of fire, I ran away from the house to protect my family. Of course, it helped to know I was one of the fastest kids in the city, all-city and all-state in track. Writing this down has helped me do a little psycho-analysis on myself and led me to realize that all I ever wanted to do in life was protect people.

Why? It hit me like a ton of bricks. I cried as I thought about my feelings, watching my dad hitting my mom when he was drunk. All I wanted to do was protect her. There it was, finally, the real reason I was so passionate about protecting people. It was me, protecting my mom when I was a child. I had thought my greatest desire in life was to love and be loved, but I guess one of the greatest acts of love is in protecting someone else.

You wouldn't know me by a cape or a red suit. Nor would you recognize me by a badge on my chest and a gun on my hip. I was just a guy in a suit, quietly behind the scenes somewhere, fulfilling my life's purpose of protecting people. I wasn't exactly a fireman, but I was putting out fires—financial fires.

It's not the kind of job you read about in the newspaper or hear about on TV. You wouldn't (until now, of course) read about how I saved hundreds of people from financial ruin or put dozens of criminals in prison for stealing millions of dollars. I'm not really comparing what I did to what police officers and firemen do, who put their lives on the line for others every day. No one was shooting at me, although I'm sure some wanted to. But it felt good to save someone's financial life.

Nearly everyone in the company looked at compliance as a necessary evil and an aggravation. Reps often saw it as something that took them away from selling and making more money. But my little back-office job was making a difference. It didn't have the kind of title that would make people stand up and take notice, like a doctor, lawyer, or fireman. But I felt good about what I was doing.

Something bad in my life put something good in my heart. I didn't just have a job now, I had a mission: to protect as many people as I could. And I used my little back-office job to do it.

CHAPTER 4

Forged by Fire

THE SEC HAD ordered Olde Stock Broker's to hire compliance officers, and one of those officers was me, Regional Vice President of Compliance. My first day on the job, I rode the elevator with a scrunchy-looking old man smoking a fat stogie. It turned out to be Mr. Olde himself. He was a fine example of what I would find in the rest of the company.

Mr. Olde, the President and CEO, ran his broker-dealer like a cross between a sweatshop and an assembly line. The headquarters was an old dilapidated building located in downtown Detroit, Michigan. Judging by the way people were dressed, it didn't appear they had a dress code. The back-office people made minimum wages, and their jobs were all broken down into very small slivers of the work, so almost no one knew how all the pieces fit together or the job of the person sitting across from them. That made it easy for them to fire anyone and quickly replace them.

The only difference between this place and the factory where I used to work was I didn't smell like oil every day. But it was just as dirty.

The employees cared little about their jobs and had no pride in their company or their work. They yelled, screamed, and cussed at reps on the phone all day. What's worse, that attitude spilled over to the reps, who in turn, yelled and screamed at their clients. I had never seen such disrespect and disregard for other people. Olde reps were known for their "churn 'em and burn 'em" attitudes. They seemed to thrive on that mentality. I once had to discipline a rep because, in one single month, he took a $300,000 account, turned it into a $200,000 account, and made $100,000 in commissions at the same time.

They all reminded me of a poem I'd like to share:

The unwilling
Led by the unqualified
To do the unnecessary
For the ungrateful.

My mission was to search for and stop any abusive activity by reps. My office was in Richmond, Virginia, and I was handling the entire East Coast. First, though, I trained at headquarters in Detroit for a couple of months, where a lady named Kim trained me on their systems.

I told her one day, "You're too beautiful to be having those cussing words coming out your mouth. If you spoke to the reps with a little more respect, you might get a much better response." That kind of language seemed to be the norm around there. I couldn't wait to move to Richmond.

But it was no better there. My first day in the Richmond office, I just walked around for a while and observed the reps. I couldn't believe how unprofessional they were, even in front of clients. I saw guys with multi-colored shirts, with pulled down ties and their sleeves rolled up with a pack of cigarettes tucked into them. One young lady wore a pair of six-inch stiletto heels with a thin wrap-around dress that exposed everything but her price tag. I'm still not sure what she was selling.

A couple of guys were throwing a football back and forth. There was a giant flowerpot sitting at the front door that had at least three years' worth of cigarette butts in it and around it.

For ten minutes, not one person asked if they could help me. They ignored me like I was a piece of furniture. One rep was yelling at a client on the phone, telling him he was stupid if he wasn't following his advice and that he didn't appreciate the client wasting his time placing orders for less than a thousand shares. He yelled, "I make money for my clients! You give me a call when you decide you want to make money too!" Then he slammed the phone down so hard you could hear it outside the building. It was more like a frat house than a professional brokerage firm. I was thoroughly disappointed.

One rep finally asked if he could help me. He smelled like he had drunk his lunch at a brewery. I told him I was looking for the manager.

He said the manager was on the phone but he would be right with me. The manager wasn't actually expecting me until the next morning, so I quietly left.

What a disaster. I certainly had my work cut out for me. Early the next morning, I showed up again for the meeting which I had set up over the phone. You should have seen their faces when I walked in. I'm sure they knew I was coming because the construction people had been building my office for about three weeks. But it wasn't the "Oh my God, he's black" look. It was the "Oh shit, this was the guy who was here yesterday" look.

The manager introduced me: "This is Loyall Wilson, the new Regional Vice President of Compliance from the home office."

I started off saying, "This office will be the flagship office for the East Coast. While I report day-to-day to the chief compliance officer, I answer to the SEC. I was sent here to make some much-needed changes, and those changes will start immediately.

"I'm authorized to terminate anyone I feel is compromising the integrity of this firm and our clients. I will review every rep who works here—and all their clients. I have a formula I use to calculate the turnover ratio in a client's account. If you exceed that ratio you'll get a warning, and if you continue, I will remove that account and/or terminate you. Any questions?"

The room was dead quiet.

"Let's talk a little about my expectations for your conduct in this office. Judging by the cigarette butts out front, a lot of you smoke.

When I walked up to the office yesterday, you looked like a gang of hoodlums, standing around smoking and cussing. I want that giant ashtray moved to the back of the building and all those butts swept up. If you have to smoke, you take it out back.

"This office is not a playground, so I don't want to see you playing football or any other games in here. Clients come to this office, so you will look and act professionally at all times. When the market is closed, there are no clients in here and the doors are locked, you can do whatever the hell you want.

"The SEC is looking at how we conduct business, so we also have to change that, or we won't be in business. I've already run some analyses on where I know some of you have churned some clients' accounts, and I will interview the reps I have concerns about. I know this is a lot to take in but we will get through this and we will be better off because of it.

"I know some of you are thinking that as soon as possible, you'll try to transfer to another office. I can assure you it won't matter where you are sitting, my reach extends to every office on the East Coast.

"One last thing. What you do on your own time is your business. But if you go out and down three or four beers for lunch, and come back to work smelling like a brewery, you will be sent home."

This branch was an example of what I saw in almost every branch I visited over the next couple of years. I fired about twenty reps that first year alone. But nothing I did was enough to save the company.

In the end, Mr. Olde was booted out of the industry and fined $5,000,000. Olde Stock Brokers was eventually sold to H&R Block. So the job in Minnesota must have been God's way of letting me know it was time to move on.

CHAPTER 5

Back to the Snow

AS I SAID, the president took a chance and hired me. I might not have really been looking for a job, but he made me an offer I couldn't refuse. So I bought a heavy coat and moved to Minnesota, also known as *Minn-e-snow-ta* or *Minn-e-so-cold-a*.

I quickly found out why the pot was so sweet. The president had fired two of his compliance officers and the other two had quit. The reason this was significant was that FINRA rules dictate that every major branch of a firm must be audited at least once a year and every registered rep must have a face-to-face compliance meeting with a compliance officer, also once a year. Well, it was June then, and not one of the fifty-two branches had been audited. And not one of the twenty-two hundred reps had their compliance meetings—and, by the way, those twenty-two hundred reps were scattered across all fifty-two states. Needless to say, I was going to be busy.

I'll give you a little background on how their system was set up. Our field force/registered reps and the offices/branches they worked out of were all independently owned and operated.

They all had contracts to work with us and sell our products. All registered reps must be associated with a broker-dealer, and that broker-dealer is charged with supervising them.

Registered reps must be properly licensed to sell certain products. For example, to sell life insurance you must be licensed to sell insurance in each state you do business in. To sell securities, you must be licensed under FINRA. To sell stocks, you must have a Series 7 license. To sell mutual funds and variable life insurance, you must have a Series 6. To supervise reps, you need the appropriate principal's license: Series 26 or Series 24.

One of the first things I had to do was to make sure everyone was properly licensed. I didn't think this would be a problem until I realized two of the largest firms were not on my list to audit. When I asked why, I was told they were classified as a branch because the managing partners of those branches were not properly licensed. This turned out to be a huge problem because half the managing partners in the system were not properly licensed to supervise their own offices. Even the home-office regional vice presidents, the very people I would be sending out to enforce the rules, were not properly licensed.

Remember when I mentioned that most salespeople don't like compliance? How do you think they felt when the new guy came in and told them they had to take the exams to get their proper licenses or else they'd no longer be paid on certain product sales? Needless to say, it didn't go over very well.

The day after I sent a memo out to the field informing them of the requirements, the vice president of sales and marketing stopped me in the hallway, yelling and screaming like a madman. Well, I guess he was mad. But it was a funny sight because he stood about six-eight and I stood on a chair at about five-five. He told me he had not given his approval for that memo to go out to the field.

As I said earlier, in order to supervise registered reps and the registered products they sell, you must be a registered principal, which he was not. I told him, right to his chest, "I would only need your approval if one, you were a principal and two, if you were the chief compliance officer. And I'm pretty sure you're neither." He was so shocked that he didn't even have a comeback. He just stood there with this dumb look on his face as I walked away.

As a result of my memo, the chairman received letters from the top four managing partners, saying I should be terminated. But the chairman backed me all the way, telling the partners they could not come to him complaining about a NASD or SEC rule when all they had to do was take a test to comply with those rules.

It helped that I had sent him a heads-up letter letting him know what I was doing. I also sent him a copy of the NASD rules that required those licenses and a warning letter from the SEC and NASD reprimanding our firm for failing to comply with those rules. That letter was dated four years before I even started working there. I guess it got lost in someone's files.

Four of the top managing partners in the system had rebelled against me for requiring them to be properly licensed to do their jobs. I'm not sure how you argue against a rule that was made long ago by the SEC and then say I'm being unfair for enforcing it. But after finding that they weren't getting any sympathy from the chairman's office, they made a last-minute scramble to meet my deadline and pass their exams. Sometimes, the testing facilities filled up and they had to travel to another city and, in some cases, another state to find one that could accommodate them. Luckily, all four of them passed.

There were other managing partners that weren't so lucky. One, in particular, failed the exam badly. He then had to wait thirty days to sit again, but he failed again. He could try once more after another thirty days, but if he failed a third time, he would have to wait six months, and after a fourth time, he would have to wait a year before retaking it.

After he did, in fact, fail the fourth time, and didn't come within twenty points of passing, I lost all confidence that he had the ability to pass at all. Each successive failure would mean a wait of a full year before he could take the test again. That possibility was unacceptable to me. I had a three-strikes-and-you're-out rule, and he was already at four. I had to let him go.

But how was I going to have this conversation? It's not like he stole anything or wronged a client. He was a good guy with a twenty-year history with the company; he'd just entered the business when the requirements weren't so strict. But times had changed, and he wasn't changing with them.

I wanted to extend every courtesy to him, but the conversation would still be tough. It's easy to fire someone who's done something wrong. But to fire someone who had been successful in the business long before I got there because he couldn't pass a test—well, that was another story.

I told him I needed to meet with him and I would fly him in on my dime. He told me that if I was going to fire him, just do it and quit beating around the bush. I said I wanted to talk about his options and that it would be better to talk face-to-face. He agreed and flew in.

Once he was there, I told him I would allow him to stay on as a rep but he needed to give up being a managing partner. Or, I would let him resign and leave quietly with no negative announcement from my office. Only a few people in the home office knew about him failing exams, and I would make sure the information didn't get out.

In the end, he resigned and left the firm. A few years later, I ran across an article about him in the *Wall Street Journal*. He was convicted of stealing $650,000 from a client and was going to jail. Lucky for me it didn't happen on my watch. I guess he never passed the ethics part of the exam.

Would you believe that one managing partner I spoke to said he had been given an exception to the licensing requirements by the previous president of the firm? And, further, that I could not tell him how to run his own firm.

After that, it got pretty ugly. Another managing partner said, "It was bad enough that those people in Minnesota tried telling me how to run my own firm. But I'll be dammed if some nigger is going to tell me what to do." I had no idea who he was talking about, so I moved on.

Then, of course, I had to travel all over the country and do the face-to-face compliance meetings with all our reps. Welcome to the NFL. In an effort to make sure compliance didn't get out of control, the regional vice president wanted a copy of my speech and he wanted me to deliver it in front of him before we went out to do our meetings. He also gave me a list of things he wanted me to say and things I couldn't say.

I reminded him that I didn't report to him; I was the firm's compliance officer and was responsible for the content of the compliance face-to-face. The information for that meeting had to be based (per NASD rules) on an official needs assessment performed by the compliance department, and while I was open to suggestions, I would be the one to determine the content of the compliance meetings.

Keep in mind that he too was a registered rep and was required to attend a compliance meeting. It really helps to know the rules if you want to put people in their place. He was outraged at my answer and ran straight to the president's office to complain.

I needed to establish both control and cohesiveness between sales management and compliance management. Although no one in the firm believed there was such a thing as "compliance management," it was apparent to me that the tail had been wagging the dog in this company for quite some time: sales ruled. So I needed to make my presence known—not as a yes man, but as a gatekeeper, the person in charge of all regulatory supervision over every registered person in the company. Someone who was not afraid to say, "no."

This company had been very successful selling insurance for a130 years, but it was now a full-service financial company, and that world was completely different from what they were used to. The regulators had set many new boundaries around how you could sell registered products, and I needed to help bring the company and its reps up to speed quickly.

That wasn't going to be easy. Everyone in the company was always reminding me how successful they had been long before I got there. But if they wanted the same success long after I left, they would have to make some changes. I wanted them to keep succeeding, but they would have to stop looking at me as some "black guy" telling them what to do. They needed to look at me as an officer of the company, there to help lead them into the future.

The thing about being a black guy at an all-white company was that I would have to fight a lot more battles than just the ones they paid me to fight. I learned early in life that you don't demand respect, you command it. I had to act like I belonged there.

I used to ask my boss, "What do senior management think?" and his answer was always the same: "You are senior management." I just happen to be black. I don't know why people thought they had to remind me of that as if I might forget.

Even the people assisting us while traveling with the company did it. Once, I was traveling to a regional meeting with a group of officers from the company and a person was helping us collect our luggage and board a bus. As we got off the plane, someone checked our names off a list. We all stood there, giving her our names, and when I gave her mine she told me, "Your name would not be on the list, and you should go to the side and wait for instructions."

At first, I thought they had a limo waiting for me because I was so special. They didn't.

I said, "Of course my name is on the list. My name is Loyall Wilson. Would you please check the list?"

She told me again, but with attitude this time, "Your name is not on the list because we don't put drivers on the list! Now go over there and wait for instructions!"

All the other officers (who happened to be white) were standing there listening. That's when I lost it. Just a little. "I am the vice president of this company, check the fucking list!" This time I was the one with the attitude.

"I'm sorry, sir. I thought you were a driver."

I guess I was being profiled.

A Teaching Moment

Sometimes, you have to dig in like a tick and stay focused. I never let those types of things distract me from my mission to protect clients, the firm, and the reps. Success is never easy, but it comes if you stay focused on doing the right thing, follow your heart, and don't define success by your title or your paycheck. And especially don't let narrow-minded people throw you off your game. Ok, enough preaching.

CHAPTER 6

Regional Meetings

WE BROKE THE country into sections for these meetings. My first was in San Francisco. One of the regional vice presidents from the home office, Bill, took me around to introduce me.

One of the first people I met was Sam, the managing partner from Sacramento. The first thing Sam did after he shook my hand was to get in my face and chew my ass out. He let me have it for anything that had ever gone wrong with the company, with compliance, and with the entire industry. He yelled and cussed until he was blue in the face. Then it was my turn.

I told him, "First off, you need to back the fuck up out of my face. You don't know me and I don't know you. But what I do know is that you are dead wrong about the last five things you complained about."

I quoted him the rules and requirements regarding the events he'd mentioned, and told him, "You're also wrong about what was going on at other firms like Merrill Lynch and Charles Schwab, because I've worked there and I know exactly what they did and did not do."

Bill just stood there with a scared expression on his face and probably was wondering if Sam and I would come to blows.

But I wasn't worried about that. Sam had most likely never met a compliance officer or anyone else who stood his ground like that before. And I wasn't about to back down or be spoken to like that—particularly by some asshole who didn't know what he was talking about.

This was one of those moments that sets the stage for the rest of your career. You either gain the respect you need to do the job, or you take your butt home and sit down. Sam quickly realized that he wasn't dealing with your typical home-office person. He didn't see an ounce of fear in my eyes, and he quickly took a couple of steps back. In an apologetic voice, he told me that no one had explained those rules to him like that. He was sorry he lit into me that way. I smiled and didn't give it a second thought.

Given how new I was to the company, I thought I would give my boss a heads-up phone call, telling him to expect a complaint about my behavior. But he never got one. Two years later, I gave Sam the choice to voluntarily resign or be terminated for failure to follow policies and procedures I had put in place. He resigned.

Now it was time for my first speech in front of the field force. I don't think Bill quite knew how to introduce me. Either that, or he was still in shock from my conversation with Sam. All he said was, "I would like to introduce our new compliance officer." He didn't even say my name. So, I had to introduce myself.

There were about three hundred registered reps there. I could tell from their faces and comments afterward that they were quite surprised at my extensive background. They had never met a compliance officer with the sales experience I had. And I had more licenses and registrations than anyone else in the room. The fact that I had been a selling rep seemed to have a calming effect, lowering their anxiety and raising their respect for me. That was something no other compliance officer had ever achieved before. Having a good sense of humor didn't hurt either.

I explained that the world of compliance was changing, that the regulations were getting tougher because of all the bad things going on in the industry. I not only told them about the rules, I explained why those rules were made and how they applied to their business. I told them how some of those rules hadn't been applied properly at our firm and that we would have to make changes. I figured that no one had ever aired the company's dirty laundry before, but it might help them understand the logic behind the rules and accept the necessary changes.

I told them that compliance was their friend, not their enemy. "Compliance is here to help, not play '*got you.*' My staff and I will be here to answer questions. I don't mind mistakes, I know they'll happen, but it is critically important that you do not try to handle or cover up a mistake. Call me first, and I'll help you through it. You need to understand that sometimes the answer will be 'no.' But you will never get a 'no' without an explanation why. Now, I won't circumvent the rules, but I may be able to offer an alternative."

I also used humor and told them a few stories about other reps in the industry that had broken the rules and the consequences of their actions. I talked about how the company had gotten in trouble with the regulators and needed to make some serious changes. Some might be uncomfortable at first, but we would be much better off.

I told them I would be making changes to the OBA (outside business activity) approval process. Per FINRA rules, every registered rep that does business outside the scope of the firm's investment business must have approval from the firm. I gave them a real example of an OBA request that came in for approval, which I denied and received a tremendous amount of pushback for my "no" answer.

Both the regional vice president and the managing partner had approved the OBA, which came from a new rep who wanted to continue her previous job's activity while she was building her clientele. Normally that's not a problem, but in this case, her full-time job was a stripper at a local nightclub. I joked that I personally had to audit her OBA request, at her place of employment.

They laughed, and it eased the tension as I set the stage for the other things I would say no to. This was the beginning of the "King of No."

I got all kinds of questions from the reps, some good and some as dumb as they could be. One question, in particular, was interesting. A rep asked me, "What would you do if you discovered that a rep had misappropriated money from a client?"

I told him, "After I fired the rep, I would make sure we took care of the client and they got all their money back."

Many of the reps laughed because they thought a compliance officer could not get that done. I didn't know whether I had that kind of authority; I just assumed I did. Besides, it was the right thing to say. Little did I know that the questioner would later be at the center of one of the biggest investigations in the history of the company. One that would uncover an $8,000,000 Ponzi scheme. (Don't worry, I'll tell you about it later.)

The reps rated me the best speaker at the meeting and even raved that it was the best compliance meeting they'd ever had. I continued doing my dog-and-pony show across the country, with the same measure of success. News traveled fast about my approach to compliance, and they loved it.

Word got back to the home office long before I did. They welcomed my return with great appreciation for what I had accomplished, and they assured me it was no small accomplishment: they had never heard of anyone, let alone a compliance officer, receiving the compliments and accolades from the field force that I did.

I gave similar speeches to the home-office employees. I wanted them to know what I was saying out there and that they were the eyes and ears of compliance. Compliance was everyone's job, not just the compliance department. I needed to expand my team, so for all intents and purposes, I deputized the entire company. Four sets of eyes could not supervise thousands of people; I needed their help.

I told them what to look for, what was acceptable and what was not. I was putting new rules into place and informing the field force about all of them. I wanted everyone in the home office to know that if they had a problem or concern they felt uncomfortable going to their supervisor about, they could come directly to me and I would take care of it. Some supervisors were not thrilled about that bit of advice, but I needed people to know it wasn't just empty goodwill. I cared about doing the right thing and I had the strength and backing to get it done.

News traveled fast in the home offices. They had heard about me standing up to some pretty powerful people in the company and I was still standing. I got more speaking opportunities from different parts of the company. I even had H.R. ask me to speak to a group of minorities. I was honored, though I'm not sure H.R. was thrilled with what I had to say.

For example, one person asked me about my mentor. They complained that it was hard to get a mentor in the company because none of the available mentors looked like them and they wanted to know who my mentor was.

"Don't worry about a mentor looking like you," I said. "My mentor was Jesus Christ, and I don't think He looked like me. A mentor is always available, but you might have to look in other places for him or her. So, don't give up."

The H.R. representative told me it was inappropriate to say that. I told her I was just answering a direct question. It was a few years before they invited me back, but that didn't change my answer. Many people admired the fact that I didn't run away from questions.

CHAPTER 7

Assumed Authority

I RECEIVED A call one day from a young lady in Florida, looking for help. She was frustrated because she had already been passed to several people in the company who couldn't assist her. She didn't know what department she required, she just knew she needed guidance with her situation.

A Teaching Moment

Never give up when you're trying to solve a problem. Some large corporations have a lot of departments, or what we sometimes call silos because they don't always speak well with each other. A lower-level clerk you get on the phone may not always know how the dots connect. So, unless you are very specific about what your problem is, what you need, and who you need to reach, it may be difficult for the person to know where your call should go. Tell the person you need assistance and ask if anyone there might be able to help.

Back to the Story

I was quite new to the company when the call came in. She was crying on the phone, and the first thing she said was, "Please don't transfer me, I need help." Sometimes, nothing is more important than listening, so that's what I did.

She continued, "My mother passed away recently, and I'm sure she had more money than the registered representative is telling me she had. I know it was a small life-insurance policy, and I was the sole beneficiary. But, I know she had another $50,000 invested, and it seems to be missing. The rep keeps telling me he's not aware of any additional investment and has no record of the $50,000. He was nice at first, but he's stopped taking my calls and won't call me back. So I called the headquarters hoping someone could help me."

I asked her if she had any supporting documentation that would help me find this money. She told me she would gather up everything she could and send it to me. She also had a friend at the bank who would send me copies of anything she had. I told her that would be great. It might take a little time, but I would sort this out. I told her God must be looking out for her because I was the one person who could, and would, help her.

I needed to schedule an audit for that office anyway, so I just moved it up on the list. I wanted to review the reps' files without drawing suspicion to what I was looking for.

A week later, I went down to Florida to do my audit and meet Cindy, the young lady who had called. With the help of her friend at the bank, they had collected all kinds of stuff for me to go over. There were copies of the original check for $50,000 in her mother's name; copies of the back of the check, showing it had gone into a bank account in the name of the rep and had been signed off by someone I didn't know; copies of a property deed that had been in the name of the deceased client and was now in the name of the rep; and a few other incriminating pieces of paperwork.

I didn't know who Cindy's friend was, but she certainly put her neck on the line to help. It would normally have taken a room full of lawyers and a handful of subpoenas to get this type of information, and it was enough to make my case against the rep airtight. Now I knew just what to look for when I did my audit.

I stopped by the branch office to gathered as much information as I could and made copies of everything I needed. Then I took it all back to my hotel room to study, comparing what Cindy had brought me to what I had found in the files. Most reps don't give a second thought to all the stuff they keep in their files. From what I had learned, some reps hadn't had an audit in fifteen years. So they thought no one would look at their files. Someone did: everything I needed to put him away was all right there.

The next day I set up a meeting with Robert, the regional vice president who made the trip with me, Dean, the managing partner for the office, and Sean, the registered rep on the case. I told Robert that I needed to ask Sean a few questions about something I found during my audit.

After introductions, I opened the conversation with, "I had a phone call from a young lady whose mother recently passed away. She told me she received the death benefit from her mother's life-insurance policy and was very grateful. Then she told me that her mother had an additional $50,000 that seemed to be missing."

Sean jumped in. "I know who you're referring to. Mrs. Walker was my client. But her daughter is confused in thinking she had more money invested with me. She kept calling me, sometimes ten times a day, and I kept telling her that her mother had no other investments with me, and maybe it was with someone else. She became such a nuisance I had to stop taking her calls. I think she's so depressed that she just needs someone to talk to. But that's all this is, just a mistake on her part. I'll call her and clear this all up."

Trust but verify. That's the way I do business and you should too. Some reps have the gift of gab. They try to limit your questions to one or two, then pacify you with a smooth answer that will satisfy your concerns. But I've been here many times before and I was just getting started.

I said, "Let me ask you a few questions, just to clear up something in my own mind. What's the name of your DBA?"[1]

"Turner Investments."

"I have a copy of a check made out to Mrs. Walker for $50,000. On the back of the check are Mrs. Walker's signature and the signature of someone named Olivia Buckner. Do you know who that is?"

---

1 DBA: "doing business as"

"That was my assistant," Sean said.

"How can I get in touch with her?" I asked.

"She ah … passed away."

Dean jumped in. "Mrs. Buckner was Sean's mother. What the hell is this all about? I know you're not coming into this office and accusing him of any wrongdoing. You have no right to question his integrity. I've known Sean for thirty years. We started the business together."

Robert must have thought it was time to put his two cents in, so he said, "Look, I can vouch for Sean as well. Now, he told you he would call Cindy and clear all this up, so you need to just drop it."

"I'll drop it when I'm finished. Now, I'm not accusing anyone of anything, but I expect Sean to answer my questions. I have a young lady who says her mother's money is missing, and I expect to find an answer for her. Now let me finish. Sean, why would your mother be signing off on the back of Mrs. Walker's check?"

"I don't know," he said. "Maybe she and my mother went into some kind of business together. I know my mother did real estate on the side."

I felt sick to my stomach. This asshole was about to blame this on his deceased mother. "Why was the money deposited in your bank account?"

"What do you mean, my account? Why would you say that?"

"Take a look at the account number on the back of the check. Do you recognize it?"

"Why the hell would I recognize it? I don't know whose account number that is. How in the hell did you get this, anyway?"

I told him. "According to the bank, it's your account number."

He became quiet and lowered his head.

I said, "You know, I think I have enough information for now. I'm going to have you suspended and prosecuted for stealing $50,000 from Mrs. Walker. When I get back to Minnesota, I'll send a report to the NASD, and you'll most likely be booted out of the industry."

Both the managing partner and the regional VP went crazy,

screaming at the top of their lungs. I could barely make out what they were saying, except that I had no authority to do this.

I stood up and walked away.

Robert ran up behind me yelling, "I'm the supervisor for registered reps in the field and *I* decide what action will be taken regarding them!"

"Oh, you might be the supervisor for sales matters, but I'm the supervisor over all registered reps for compliance matters—and that includes *you.*"

That didn't sit well with him. So he put on his salesmen's hat and said in a very calm (let me try this another way) voice, "Let's talk about this. I'm sure we can come up with a satisfactory way to take care of it."

I said, "As long as it includes him paying the money back and being terminated, I am willing to listen."

Then his voice rose again. "I'm pretty sure you don't have that authority!"

"Then I guess we'll see how much authority I have," I said. Then I went to the nearest phone and called, Tom, one of the members of my team. I told him to suspend Sean's securities license for misappropriating money from a client's account, and I would fill out the paperwork when I returned to the office. He asked me if I had approval from Bob, the president, to do that.

"No, Bob didn't hire me to ask his approval every time I need to do something. So please, suspend his license or tell me how to do it and I'll do it myself."

Next, I called Bob to let him know what I had done. All he said was, "Good job. I'll handle any fallout on this end."

I never asked his permission, and he never said I didn't have the authority. So, I assumed that I did.

That evening, I had dinner with Robert and Dean. Dean told me that Sean had confessed everything to him.

"First," he said, "I would like to apologize for my behavior earlier. I didn't know how to react because Sean and I have been so close over the years, and there was no way I could believe he'd do something like that. But I've learned my lesson—to never say never.

"He admitted it all. He's so sorry. I watched him cry in my office for twenty minutes. He realizes he's made a huge mistake and he wants to make amends. So, because of our history, I have to ask you this: Is there any way we can resolve this short of termination and prosecution?"

My answer was, "No, you don't get to steal money from a client, pay it back and think it's all good." The rest of the dinner was conspicuously quiet.

The next morning, I called Cindy and told her what had happened. She was very happy and thanked me for everything I'd done. Meanwhile, I apologized that she had to go through so much hassle just for the right thing to happen.

Things are never as easy as they should be. I fired Sean. I took the money back from his commissions, and the NASD banned him from the industry for life. But we could never prosecute him. Apparently, when the police went looking for him, he hid on an Indian reservation, and he's never been found. I don't imagine you make it onto the FBI's most-wanted list for small white-collar crimes.

One thing for sure, no one questioned whether I have the authority again.

CHAPTER 8

Q. What Do You Give a Crying Rep?
A. "Exceptions"

ONE DAY, I was sitting in my office and heard this commotion in the hallway. Apparently, a rep had brought a young back-office clerk to tears by yelling at her over the phone when he called in some trades. The trades on their own should not have been a problem, but in this case, the client was deceased. Julie, the back-office clerk knew it was wrong and refused to place the trades. The rep went over her head, and her supervisor gave him an 'exception' and told the back-office person to place the trades.

A Teaching Moment

It is against SEC rules to trade in a single-name account if the named person is deceased. In order to trade in the account, you need certain court documents appointing a representative.

Back to the Story

The back-office person had heard me mention this in one of my talks, so she knew the rules and tried to explain them to the rep. But because this was a high-producing rep, the supervisor felt it was more important to find a way to say yes (as she had done so many times in the past).

I asked Julie to bring me all the information on the account, then get the rep on the phone. I put the phone on speaker so Julie could hear what was going on. The rep's assistant answered the phone and told me the rep was busy and would have to get back to me later.

"No problem," I said. "Be sure to inform him that all his trades are being canceled and that he can call me whenever he gets a moment."

I guess he got un-busy because he got on the phone right away.

"Do you know who I am?" he said.

"No, I don't."

He yelled about who he was and how much money he had made for the company, and if his orders were not placed, he would have my ass fired before the end of the day. His name was Bert.

I politely told Bert, "I don't know who you are, and I don't care how much money you've made for the firm. Let me ask you this: Who gave you the orders to be placed in this account?"

"The client."

"I would like to speak to the client to verify these orders."

He said, "You know the client is deceased."

"So when did you get the orders from the client?"

"We talked before he died."

"Do you have proof of that?"

"No."

"Well, in that case, let me explain to you what will happen. All the trades you placed today have been canceled. I will flag this account so that no trades can be placed without my personal approval, and that won't happen until I receive all the proper court documents."

Bert asked me, "Who is your boss?"

"I report to the president."

"Then you need to transfer me to him, right now."

"Of course, not a problem. But I should tell you in advance, that no matter who you speak to, you don't get to trade in a dead person's account, and the president will not intervene on your behalf. What he will do is tell you that I am the chief compliance officer for this firm, and these types of things fall under my jurisdiction. Then he will refer you back to me." And with that, I transferred the call.

This was just the first of many run-ins with Bert over the next couple of years. It finally came to a head when he sent letters out to his clients, requesting that they, in turn, write letters of complaint to the home office about the "asshole" in compliance disrupting trading activity. Of, course, he denied doing that until I produced a copy of the letter with his signature on it.

After a little coaching on the part of senior management, Bert joined another broker-dealer.

A couple of good things came out of this exchange. The back-office person felt a sense of redemption and pride. Through me, she had won a battle against a powerful registered rep who was wrong and who didn't get his way because of who he was or through intimidation. She had someone stand behind her when she was right. She also learned that getting to "yes" is not as important as getting to the right answer, which in this case was "no."

I could tell that the supervisor who gave the exception was a little upset. I know she wanted to be accommodating whenever possible because that was the company's way. For the first time in her career, her authority had been questioned. She had been overruled by someone who was not her boss. But my decisions were based on rules, not accommodations.

It was not her fault she thought this way. She'd grown up in a system built on exceptions. The bigger you were and the more you produced, the more exceptions you were allowed. She had been taught the broker-dealer's number-one job was to process business submitted by the field force.

Exceptions were used as a way to appease the selling reps in the field that relied on them and developed a sense of entitlement as a result. The regulatory world was changing, and we had to change with it. Exceptions should be a rare occurrence, not an everyday way of life. If you make exceptions in every situation, why have the rule in the first place? I had to show the back-office team that if the right answer was "no," they shouldn't be afraid to give it, nor should they be afraid of being overruled because of who the rep was.

Most reps were very understanding when they were educated about the rules, why they were in place, and most importantly how they protected clients, the firm, and the reps themselves.

When a business decision is made without an understanding of the rules, it's a step along the road to disaster. For example, someone once gave a managing partner an exception to trade on margins when he wasn't licensed to do so. He lost hundreds of thousands of dollars for his clients, and we were responsible for the losses.

Someone else wanted to make our application more pleasing to the eye, so they left off the arbitration clause. As a result, we got into trouble for not following NASD rules requiring that clause; it also left us open to thousands of potential lawsuits (The arbitration clause is an agreement between the client and the company which state that both parties will resolve any disputes in front of an arbitration panel instead of seeking resolution in court).

I always have tons of email and phone calls from people trying to get exceptions for things they shouldn't be doing. One time, a call came in from a managing partner. My team had rejected one of the candidates he wanted to hire to become a registered rep.

He told me the candidate had got into a little trouble when he was young. He said it was one of those dumb college pranks, and he had been caught smoking weed in the dorm. I'm not an unreasonable person, and I know people make mistakes. I asked him to send me the information and I would take a look at it. Remember what I said about "trust but verify."

As I looked over the information, something seemed to be missing, so I had my team order me the official police report of the incident. It turned out the candidate was now twenty-two; it had happened when he was twenty-one. That wasn't the picture I had in mind when he said, "It happened when he was younger," although it was technically true.

The "college prank," according to the police report, involved the man being charged with 1. possession of an illegal substance with the intent to sell, 2. possession of an illegal firearm, and 3. armed robbery. That's one hell of a college prank.

Like most managing partners and most reps, he wanted to see how far I could be pushed. He yelled and screamed for a while, and he threatened to go over my head to the chairman. These things don't really bother me, so I told him I'd transfer his call to the chairman, so he could report I'd refused to hire a convicted felon. With that, I transferred him and hung up. I think he was still talking. I later heard he was going around blaming me for his inability to meet his hiring goals because I kept rejecting his candidates.

Oh well.

Outside of a few dinosaurs walking around not realizing they were extinct, the perception of compliance had changed. I had been invited to sit on the boards of a few of our smaller companies. Compliance now had a seat at the table for all the company's major decisions. Managing partners also invited me to speak at their branch meetings. People in the industry were taking notice and inviting me to speak at industry meetings. The world was getting "compliance fever." Which was a good thing. New reps were joining the firm because of our high compliance standards.

My team and I were making a difference. I'd been promoted a few times and was making very good money. The compliance unit had grown from four people to thirty-two. My budget had grown tenfold and my responsibilities continued to expand. I was a long way from my robot days on the line at Ford.

I had gained a reputation for being hard but fair. Remember the sales goal of "getting to yes"? It was now more like "getting to yes when appropriate." There was far less pushback when I had to deliver a no. The buck no longer stopped at the president's office; it stopped at mine. If someone on my team said no, it usually meant that I would say no, too. Very few people were going over my head, and my team felt more empowered to do their jobs. Compliance was becoming the training ground for the firm's future leaders. I had told over five thousand people that compliance was everybody's responsibility. And they responded. Here's one example.

Per FINRA rules, if someone committed a financial crime in some other capacity, they could be statutorily disqualified from working in a broker-dealer. In fact, even if the person wasn't registered and only worked in the office as an assistant or mail person, they fall under these requirements.

One of our registered reps, Harold, was at a party one night. He ran into his managing partner's assistant, Heather. They had a drink and talked for a while, then she went on her way. Later, one of Harold's friends asked him how he knew Julie.

Harold said, "I don't know anyone named Julie."

"For someone who didn't know her, you seemed pretty friendly with her."

Harold said, "Are you talking about Heather, with the long black hair?"

"No, I'm talking about Julie, with the long black hair, who I went to school with."

Harold was confused. "I know her as Heather. We've worked together for five years."

They continued to compare notes. The next day, Harold told his managing partner, Glenn, about the incident. Then they both called me right away. Glenn told me that Heather had been his assistant for close to ten years, that she was an excellent employee and he didn't want to get her in trouble, but he felt he needed to call me in on this.

I requested all the personal information he had on Heather so I could run a background check on her. I turned that information over to Terry, one of my top investigators, to fill in the blanks.

A brief aside: Terry used to be a detective for the Chicago Police Department. He was one of the first guys to uncover insurance fraud after the 9–11 incident in New York. As a company, we tried to be sensitive to the politically charged situation of that time, and because so many bodies couldn't be identified, we couldn't always follow normal procedures when paying out life-insurance benefits to the beneficiaries. We wanted to hand deliver the checks, but as a precaution, we would send Terry to give his final blessing before we released them.

Terry used a technique he had perfected, where he went around the neighborhood of the deceased asking unthreatening questions like, "Do you know the family? I hear she's a great mom." Anything that would get them talking—people love to brag about their friends. When he asked at one grocery store about the family, an employee was very helpful and told him that Nancy and the kids were just in the store earlier that day. Nancy, according to our claims form, had died in the 9–11 building collapses. As you can imagine, that situation took a quick turn in a completely different direction.

Anyway, back to Heather/Julie. Terry quickly determined that they were one and the same. Julie had committed armed robbery and burglary when she was seventeen. (This, by the way, falls under my definition of a dumb mistake when you're young.) She was thirty-four now and going by the name of Heather. She had been using a fake social-security number that had gone undetected. Even though she wasn't registered, I had a rule in place that anyone in the office who processed checks or certificates had to be fingerprinted, and those prints would go through our normal clearance check. Someone must have made a mistake somewhere because nothing had ever come up. I believe the prints were taken but never submitted. Either way, she had grown into a responsible adult, and the managing partner felt she had earned an opportunity to start over. I agreed.

So, congratulations to the lady with the long black hair. Whoever you are.

One salesperson thought it would be nice if managing partners could collect premiums from clients, deposit the money in one large account, and then write checks out of the account when necessary to pay premiums for the clients. Not only did this violate the NASD comingling rules, it allowed reps to steal millions of dollars from clients. (I'll share some of those stories later.) Once the company realized they were in violation of the NASD rules, they set out to make sure all those accounts were closed. I discovered, in some old compliance files, that my predecessors had sent a questionnaire to the managing partners asking if they had used the special account and, if they had, to please acknowledge that they had closed it.

I guess that's part of the "Minnesota nice" thing I always hear about. Maybe it's true that Minnesotans are very nice people, but they seemed to have forgotten that the company hired reps from all over the country who might not be "Minnesota nice."

Anyway, all the partners had returned the form and answered the question with a "yes." I am a firm believer in the philosophy of "trust but verify." I may have been the only one in the company who lived by that rule because I found no evidence that anyone had actually verified these statements were true. The company asked, the partners answered yes, and the company accepted it. But it turned out not all these answers were true and some of the untrue answers open the door to some reps stealing millions of dollars for clients.

CHAPTER 9

Two for One

WHILE DOING A routine audit in Massachusetts, I was going over one of the rep's commission statements when I noticed the lines on one of his statements seemed to be a little uneven and the font size on some numbers seemed a little off. I called the home office to have copies of the official statements faxed over to me so I could make a comparison.

My mistake was I should have stood next to the fax machine when they were coming in.

That evening, I went to dinner with a couple of the top reps in the office. The managing partner was supposed to join us but had to cancel at the last moment. I left my rental car at the office and rode with one of the reps, so after dinner, he dropped me back at the office to get my car. That's when I ran into the managing partner, who dropped a large storage box when he saw me. His face said it all when some of the statements I had asked for also fell onto the ground from the box.

I told him he had no right to remove items from the office in the middle of an audit, and I grabbed the box.

He immediately started justifying and making excuses for his actions. He must have been very nervous because he rambled on about how he was not being compensated enough for all the work he was doing, and his expenses were growing every day.

I said, "I know nothing about your pay structure or your expenses running this office. If you have problems like that, you should discuss them with senior management." (Oops, I forgot I was senior management). "My job is to make sure you follow all the rules and regulations and take appropriate action if you don't."

He asked me, "What kind of action?"

"You heard my compliance talk. If it turns out you were stealing money from clients or the firm, you'll be terminated and go to jail."

"I wasn't stealing money," he said. "That money was mine to use as I saw fit."

"I don't know anything about that. I just know I'm going to have a team of forensic accountants go through these statements, and we will get to the bottom of this."

I learned I have to be careful when I'm on someone else's turf and they've been caught with their hands in the cookie jar. I didn't like the way this conversation was going, so I grabbed the box and put it in my car, then headed back to my hotel to call my boss with my suspicions.

The next morning, I went to the office and found his administrative assistant crying her eyes out. The managing partner had gone home the night before and killed himself. Oh my God. I had never imagined anything like this happening.

Our accountants later confirmed my suspicions. He had stolen $2,000,000 from clients and his own reps. Of course, the corporate attorneys insisted I used the term "misappropriated." I guess with white-collar crime, it's called misappropriating, while with other criminals, it's called stealing. You call it what you will. I call it stealing but either way neither one should be punishable by death.

The ironic thing was that this managing partner had a $2,000,000 life-insurance policy written by us, on himself. Also, the non-contestability clause had expired, meaning we had to pay his wife as the beneficiary of the policy. So, he stole $2,000,000, and we had to give his wife $2,000,000. But this was not the result's either one of us wanted.

I guess I was bitten by the "Minnesota nice bug" Because I didn't feel comfortable going after the wife, even though I had evidence she was a cosigner on the "special account" that had been used to steal the money (you know, the one where the managing partners marked the box "yes" to say they were closed).

CHAPTER 10

The Ph.D.

SOMETIMES IT'S HARD to see the forest for the trees and sometimes it's hard to see the bad things if you don't look. Then there are times, when you are a sales manager, you have what is known as an "inherent conflict of interest," when you are asked to increase sales and supervise a rep at the same time. This company was committed to doing the right thing, but it was also committed to building a close relationship with the reps. That's where compliance comes in, we were the gatekeepers and we didn't have sales goals.

The regional vice presidents handled most of the complaints about reps and their business—though I would soon change that process—and the registered reps worked for the local firms that were owned and operated independently and run by a managing partner. One of these partners was David.

David was one of the most respected and trusted managing partners in our system. He had been with the company for more than twenty years, had a Ph.D., and had written several books on investing. He was also the assistant pastor of one of the largest churches in the community.

A couple of reps were unhappy about their arrangements with David, so they called the home office to complain. They wanted to go out on their own and open a firm themselves. David was totally against this and lobbied the home office to support his decision not to allow it. The reps applied a little pressure to get their way: they sent an anonymous letter—of course, we knew it was them—complaining about unethical business practices by David. The home office had a meeting to discuss the allegations, and to my complete surprise, they invited me to attend.

I informed the group that David's office was, in fact, due an audit. I could go down and investigate, under the guise of a surprise audit, and that way he wouldn't think the reps were the source of the information—just in case it turned out to be false.

From the expression on their faces, you would have thought I'd said I was going in with an AK-47 to just start shooting people to get answers. The regional vice president informed me that surprise audits were against company policy.

"Are you kidding me?" I challenged. "If I suspected a crime was being committed in an office, I'd have to call them first to tell them I was coming? As soon as I'm able, I'm going to change that policy."

Bill, the regional VP, said, "Regardless, it's the policy right now. You can go down and do the audit, but we will be calling David to let him know you are coming."

As soon as the meeting was over, I went to the corporate general-counsel's office. He told me that many processes and policies arose because a precedent had been set, even though they might not be written policies. I asked him if precedents could be changed. He said yes, but it would be a good idea to inform the field of the changes first.

That wasn't a problem. Two days later, I sent out a memo informing the field that every office, on a rotating basis, would be subject to an unannounced audit at least once every two years. Of course, the cards and letters rolled in, and none of them were happy.

Meantime, they informed David that I would do a routine audit. They said it would take a couple of hours, and he should try to accommodate me. Later, they were shocked to learn I had booked my hotel for three days.

I had my team start some behind-the-scenes background checks and some auditing of his statements, finances, and bank accounts.

I arrived at his office two days later. It was an incredibly beautiful place, with artwork that looked like it was worth thousands of dollars. He had an oak desk the size of two large desks and a stereo on the bookshelf. I had seen that stereo system a magazine and I knew cost around $5,000. It was the kind you might have in your house, but certainly not in your office. He also had a wall full of plaques showing his accomplishments: a discharge certificate from the U.S. Army, degrees from the universities he had attended, and, of course, his Ph.D. certificate.

As I was looking at the Ph.D., I thought of when my younger brother, Rennie got his "Ph.D." My mom called me just after I went to California to tell me the news. The thing is, Rennie was five years younger than me. He was very smart, so his getting a Ph.D. would have been no surprise, but oddly that was the first I heard of him even going to college. I also had a few friends who went straight to college from high school, and none of them had Ph.Ds. yet, so the math made me a little skeptical. Plus, my brother spent his three years after high school in the Navy. I told my mom what I thought, and she got upset and accused me of hating on my brother. She said I should be ashamed of myself and should be proud of him for what he had accomplished, not jealous. She was right though. I should be proud of him. And I was. Well, as it turned out, he *had* got his Ph.D. … well, a P.H.D.—which stood for Professional Hair Dresser.

I'm just saying a lot of things about David didn't add up. David had a Mercedes-Benz, a Jaguar, an Escalade, two airplanes, and two fifty-five-foot boats.

He had planned the entire itinerary for my visit, starting with lunch, dinner, and ending the evening with a hockey game. I didn't even know they had hockey in Mississippi. To no one's surprise, at the game, his name was plastered all over the stadium. The numbers were not adding up, but the regional VP told me that David had married into money. Unfortunately, no one verified whether that was true or not.

Who was this guy? He prayed before meetings, before lunch, and before dinner. He had a bible in his car and on his desk. Oh, he was certainly laying it on thick. Remember the red flags? Well, they were flying and flapping everywhere. David even became a little offended when I turned down the round of golf he had set up at a private club for the next morning. I think his plan was to keep me busy doing everything but the audit.

He was surprised when I told him I would be there for three days and would interview reps in the office. He told me that his last audit only lasted about an hour, and he didn't understand what I would do that took that long. I simply told him I would do an audit that mimicked an NASD audit, because that was the proper way to do an audit, and that I couldn't comment on how the previous compliance officers worked.

The next morning, he set me up in an office and said his assistant would provide me with anything I needed. I spoke to the entire office and gave them my compliance speech. David introduced me and told everyone to help in any way possible. I thanked him for the use of the office and started my work.

First, I had his assistant point me to the files. She said David had told her she was to pull the files for me. I told her that wasn't necessary and that I would pull them myself. Within twenty minutes, David was in my office asking how I was doing.

He could see some files on my desk, and his helpful smile quickly transformed into a look of worry and agitation. He asked me, "Why are you pulling files yourself? That's what my assistant is for. I insist that you let her do that."

"Thank you, but I'll pull my own files."

"This is my office, these are my employees, and I paid for everything in here. I won't have you going through any personal files not related to my investment business."

"Any files in this registered office will be open to my review," I told him.

"I'll see about that!" he yelled. "I'm placing a call to Minnesota right now!"

I had procured a list of names from an inside source, and I was going through those files. I could tell that some information was missing as I continued my review. Then I asked an office administrator why certain documents weren't in the files. She said she didn't know why because they were normally there.

As I was going through the incoming check blotters, I noticed a copy of a check from a client for $50,000. A note was attached saying, "sent to client in error." The check was endorsed on the back by the client for redeposit into the client's account. When I called the home office, they had no record of that check being redeposited in the client's account. The client's file in the office also had no mention of a request to order out the check. But the files in the home office showed David had ordered the check.

I phoned the client to do a quality control/customer satisfaction-type call. She was very happy with the service she was receiving from David and gave him high praise. She also told me he had called her about the mistake—that the home office in Minnesota had sent the check out in error. David had her sign the back of the check and then went to her house to pick it up as a customer-service gesture for our mistake.

As I continued my research, I found several similar situations involving checks sent out in error. An office staffer told me that errors of this kind happened a lot at the Minnesota office. Another red flag.

A Teaching Moment

If you ever receive a check that has been withdrawn from your account in error, and you return it to the local office and the registered rep asks you to endorse it on the back, that is a red flag. If it was truly sent out in error, they wouldn't need your signature to return it to your account.

Always, check your statement to see if it reflects the withdrawal and the deposit of the check. If you return the check and suddenly receive a summary statement produced by the rep—rather than an official statement produced by the broker-dealer—it's a red flag.

Clients are often concerned about receiving four or five differ- ent statements, and the rep may offer to send you only a summary statement.

That might seem fine, and a lot easier for you, but you must take the time to compare your summary statement with your official state- ment to make sure they match. Never tell the rep you want to stop receiving those annoying statements. They exist for your protection.

Back to the Audit

A few of the names I was looking for had no files. I asked the administrator about these files and was told they no longer existed. I asked if they were clients of the firm, and she said they had been but she believed they had taken their files with them when they left. I told her clients are entitled to a copy of their files, but the firm is required by law, to retain those files themselves for six years.

The next day, David came into the office in a fit of rage. He had heard I called some of his clients.

"You have no right to call my clients. They belong to me, and you have no right to question them. As a matter of fact, I want you out of my office immediately."

"If you put me out before I finish my audit, your license to do business will be suspended before I reach my car. While you service these clients, the regulatory supervision belongs to the firm, and per your contract, they are the firm's clients."

He reminded me he was one of the top-producing managing part- ners in the company and one of the most respected people in the community, whose reputation was beyond reproach.

In the eyes of a sales manager, when they look at a rep they see dollar signs. The more dollar signs they see, the more ChapStick they put on (because the more butt they have to kiss). But I don't wear ChapStick so I don't care about how much money they make. I have to be objective when doing my job.

He told me (like reps often do), "I'm a close friend of the chair- man, and I'm going to give him a call."

I responded, "Before you make your call, can you tell me why you seem to have so many missing files?"

"I wasn't aware of any requirement to retain those files after a client leaves the firm."

"That's strange, because every year on your annual questionnaire, you certify that you are aware of those requirements. But no matter. I spoke to a number of clients who're going to send me copies of their files."

When he heard that, he turned white as a ghost. There's something in the eyes of a person who knows his life is about to change. All the confidence and arrogance he was so full of had quickly drained from his body. He slowly turned and left the building.

When I got back to the hotel that evening, I called my boss to tell him what I'd found. I didn't have a lot of documented proof, but I knew this guy was stealing money from clients. My research had revealed that his Ph.D. was fake and that he hadn't married into wealth. His so-called books were actually written by someone else, and he had just paid a fee to have his name on the cover as a co-writer. His name didn't even appear within the bindings, just on the removable dust cover.

I could prove that a number of checks that had gone out to the clients in error were not errors at all. David had been requesting those checks, lying to the clients, and never redepositing them. My plan was to suspend David and have a team come down to analyze the evidence. Later that evening, I got a call from one client I had spoken too. He asked me about David, and why he was moving out of his office.

I got over to David's office as fast as possible, but he was already gone. When I walked into his office the next morning, I saw that big beautiful desk of his had secret compartments. The doors with no handles were wide open. He must have stored the files in his desk when they called to give him advance notice of my arrival. David didn't show up that morning at all, but rumors were circulating about his business partner being killed in a suspicious airplane crash. Did

I mention that David owned two airplanes? His business partner was flying one of them.

These situations are always delicate because the businesses are independently owned and operated, and they sometimes own the building too. I immediately suspended David's license and sent for a team of reinforcements to help manage the situation.

The next day, the phone lines were jammed with clients and ex-clients calling about their accounts. The press had got hold of the story and were camped outside the office. A newspaper ran the headline "Compliance Officer Goes to Hockey Game with Accused Criminal."

I wonder who that was?

The home office in Minnesota got busy circling the wagons to protect its good name and its clients. The lawyers prepared for the onslaught of lawsuits. What had started as a couple of reps complaining because they wanted to move into their own office, turned out to be a $5,000,000 securities fraud case. And the Ph.D./pastor/most-respected man in the community would spend six years in prison for stealing $5,000,000 from clients.

There are always five or six parts to these situations. First, we have to discover the wrongdoing. Then there's an analysis to prove misappropriation, followed by the criminal arrest and prosecution of the registered rep. Then we try to discover which clients have been harmed and to what extent. After that, we negotiate with the clients to return the funds to them, which often turns into lawsuits. The federal regulators—whether the SEC, FINRA, or the States—one or all will scrutinize the events and decide whether they will go after the firm for negligence or failure to supervise. And of course, the regulators look at me, as the chief compliance officer responsible for the regulatory supervision of all the firm's registered representatives and agents. They decide whether I had sufficient policies and procedures in place to prevent and or detect situations like this. If I am found to be at fault, both the firm and I can be sanctioned, fined, and even suspended for failure to supervise.

The next two phases would happen simultaneously. One part of my team would find all the victims and determine how much we owed them; the other part would try to figure out how David was able to circumvent our policies and procedures and how he managed to hide his crimes for so long.

Most of the time, clients don't even know money has been stolen from them. The trust the bond between the rep and the client; it's sometimes so strong that it blinds the client to any possibility of wrongdoing by the rep. I've handled cases in which the client wouldn't even speak to us. But their attorneys would eventually send us a letter of intent to sue. In this situation, that was the case: we had dozens of people wanting to sue us. As for their attorneys, there were a couple of times after they beat me up—I mean, deposed me—that I walked out of the room thinking I had stolen the money myself.

It's difficult to understand sometimes, especially when the clients didn't need the money and had no idea it was missing until I told them. We offered to replace all their money along with interest and any market appreciation, but they sued us anyway. Don't get me wrong: a lawsuit, in and of itself, is an amazing process. I certainly understand the process and the need to have that right. But I don't always understand the results, though.

For example, one lady didn't know her money was missing because she had no need for it. She didn't find out until I told her.

I offered to do the right thing and repay her with interest and whatever she might have made if it was properly invested, but she sued us and turned her $200,000 into $1,000,000. From her point of view, that was a great return on her investment. I get that. But when a $5,000,000 thief turns into a $28,000,000 problem, I'm just not sure it's justified. But that's how it is sometimes. I don't worry about that. I focus on my mission: protect as many people as I can, even if those same people fight me along the way.

Wait, there's more. Someone, in their infinite wisdom, made the managing partner's contract so sweet that even if he stole $5,000,000 from clients, we would still owe him his bonus. We would still have to contribute to his retirement plan, even though he would be in jail.

And someone was worried that he would sue us for his back pay. I was like, "What? Don't pay him shit—let him sue us!"

But I wasn't in charge. Oh well.

David got six years in prison. Some lawsuits lasted seven years. The clients sued us, David sued us for his bonus, we sued David for restitution. We sued the bank where he deposited the checks he stole, too—he could somehow deposit checks that were made out to someone else. Yes, apparently, if I find a check on the ground made out to someone else, I can walk into a bank and cash it with no problem—or at least that's what David did, frequently. I know I sometimes catch hell trying to cash my own check, let alone someone else's. Anyway, seven years later we reached a deal with the bank.

Out of the blue one day, I got a letter from David apologizing for what he had done. He wanted my forgiveness and asked if he could speak in front of our reps during one of my compliance meetings so he could warn others about the choices he had made and how they turned his good life bad. I told him that wouldn't be necessary because I had done a pretty good job telling that story already. And the forgiveness part was between him, God, and the people he stole money from.

During one of my compliance talks, I flashed a blown-up picture of a check I had received from David as part of his restitution payment after he got out of prison. I wanted everyone to know I would not only have them put in jail for stealing from clients, I would go after them to make sure they paid us the money back. The check was $125.00 from David's job stacking boxes at Sam's Club. I was working hard to get our money back—now he only owed us $4,999,875.00.

CHAPTER **11**

The CPA

IT WASN'T BAD enough that a handful of people had to supervise thousands of registered reps, we also had to look out for dishonest clients.

One day, for instance, a client called because he hadn't been able to reach his investment-adviser rep. The client wanted to pull his money out for a closing on a new house. The back-office administrator who took the call came into my office to describe the situation to me. She explained they could not find any information on the client or the rep.

I took the call and asked the client if he had copies of his statement or any other documents of his account. He said he had all kinds—the new account form, his investment worksheet, and his receipt for the $300,000—and he would fax them over right away. But he didn't have a copy of his statement because the rep had told him that the statements only came annually.

A TEACHING MOMENT

You should know that statements are normally sent to clients monthly. Sometimes, when there's no activity They might go out on a quarterly basis. Although one exception might be fixed life insurance, there are almost no cases in which statements only go out annually.

BACK TO THE STORY

After reviewing the documents the client sent, I had my team double-check our system. They still found no information on the client or the rep. When that search returned nothing, I knew we had a fraud case in front of us.

I called the client back to ask where he had met the rep to transact their business. He gave me an address, but I had no listing of an office there. That's when I put on my *CSI* hat. You probably know the TV show *CSI: Crime Scene Investigation.* Sometimes I think I learned as much from *CSI* as I have from any of my securities exams.

I told my team to run the rep's name through our client database. We got a hit. It matched the name of one of our life-insurance policyholders. I looked up the agent who wrote that policy, and he was still a registered rep of ours. So, I called him to introduce myself. I told him right away he wasn't in trouble, but I needed to ask him a few questions.

I have to calm registered reps down right away because they get very nervous when they receive a call from the chief compliance officer.

I asked him if he was familiar with the name "Janet Thompson." He told me that Mrs. Thompson was a client he had written a life-insurance policy for a while back. She was a CPA (certified public accountant), and the two of them had a referral agreement: she would refer accounting clients who needed investment advice to him, and he would refer clients who needed accounting services to her. Next, I asked him if he was familiar with the name "Tom Jackson." He said no. Mr. Jackson was the client calling about his $300,000. I asked the rep if he had ever done any investment business with Mrs. Thompson and again he said no.

As I continued to probe, it came to light he had once tried to get her to open an investment account, but she had never followed through. He believed he left the paperwork with her, but she never called him back.

At this point, I had already informed the managing partner of my concerns. I had to be sure that the rep was not in partnership with Mrs. Thompson in any fraudulent activity, so I had the managing partner standing by to perform a quick inspection of the rep's files. Everything seemed to be fine. I told the rep he shouldn't have any conversations with Mrs. Thompson until I gave him the okay.

She was passing herself off as one of our reps and stealing her client's money. This was a highly unusual case because Mrs. Thompson was not one of our reps and Mr. Jackson was not one of our clients.

Now it was time to give Mr. Jackson the bad news. I called him and tried to gather as much information as I could from him first. But he became impatient and demanded to know where his money was. I certainly understood because it probably sounded like I was giving him the runaround.

"Mr. Jackson," I told him, "This will sound a little crazy to you but your CPA, Mrs. Thompson, is not a registered representative of our company. I believe that Mrs. Thompson has whited-out information on an old application she had for herself and used it to pass herself off as a registered rep. But she has never worked for this firm, and she is not a registered rep of any FINRA-registered broker-dealer. We don't know you as a client and have never received any money or application on your behalf, from her or anyone else.

"I believe Mrs. Thompson has stolen your $300,000. I've taken the liberty of making a few calls to the local authorities. They're expecting your call so they can advise you and give you the opportunity to press charges against her.

"My company will also make formal charges against Mrs. Thompson for impersonating one of our reps. You should get an attorney right away, and I would be happy to help you in any way I can. I am sorry that this happened to you."

I never spoke to or met Mrs. Thompson but I testified at her trial. Both she and her husband had stolen $10,000,000 from their clients. They were both sentenced to five years in prison.

A Teaching Moment

Always look for documentation to authenticate any person's claim to be a registered representative.

First, a sign should be posted in the office where the rep does business reading "Securities being offered through…" with the name of the broker-dealer. That disclosure should also be on the person's business card.

Next, you should go to the FINRA website and research the person by name. Every registered rep in the country will be listed there. If they are not, call FINRA immediately. If the person is an investment adviser rep, they will be listed in the state in which they do business or with the SEC. There are a few small exceptions to this, depending on the state.

Any time you are dealing with someone who claims to be a registered rep or an investment adviser rep, you should be able to find information on one of those websites to corroborate their claim. Just because they have their own office or their own website, doesn't mean they are who they say they are. "Trust but verify" is my motto, and it should be yours too.

CHAPTER **12**

The CUSIP Number

IT WAS A slow day at work. I think it was opening day for fishing or hunting season—it doesn't really matter which because they're both like national holidays in Minnesota. So, few people were in the office. I was going over some paperwork at my desk when one of the home-office employees working in the service center knocked at my door. She apologized for bothering me, but I have an open-door policy and it was no trouble. She said there was no one else around and she was hoping I could answer a question for a client. She had tried to help her but didn't understand the problem. The client was preparing to have her taxes done and had a question about her tax-free bond she owned.

I said of course, no problem. I told her to go ahead and transfer the client in. I suggested she stayed to hear the answer so she would be equipped to deal with a similar situation it in the future.

The client was a very nice elderly lady. After she described her problem, I asked her to give me the name of the bond, the description, and the interest rate it was paying.

I was immediately suspicious when she told me the bond was paying 9%. I wanted to be sure she was reading it correctly, so I asked her for the CUSIP number. The customer-service rep noticed my facial expression changing completely as I wrote down what I understood the client was saying.

Then I apologized to the client, telling her we had a really bad connection, and asked if she would be so kind as to fax me a copy of the bond and her statement. She said no problem; her copier had the ability to fax documents. The reason for my concern was she kept reading off a nine-digit numerical CUSIP number, when the last three digits should have been letters.

A Teaching Moment

Anytime a company or government entity issues stocks or bonds, those securities are always identified by a nine-digit CUSIP number. If it's a stock, this will be nine numbers. If it's a bond, the last three digits will be letters. CUSIP stands for Committee on Uniform Security Identification Procedures.

Back to the Story

As soon as the fax came in, I knew I was dealing with forged documents and a new financial crime. I assembled the leaders of my team and had them pull all the background information on the registered rep, his office and his managing partner. One of my managers reminded me this was the same rep who had stood up at one of my compliance face-to-face meetings and asked me what would happen if I discovered that a rep was misappropriating money from clients.

"Damn." I'd been face-to-face with a criminal who knew he was stealing money from clients. I remember telling someone, as a joke, to write that guy's name down when he asked that stupid question. I bet, when I told him we would make sure all the clients got their money back, he took that as a permission slip to keep doing what he was doing, with no worries about harming the clients and thinking he wouldn't be caught. I remember the asshole just laughed and sat down after I answered his question. But now his days were numbered. He just didn't know it yet.

I told the client on the phone, that we were having system problems, but I would actually be out there on Monday (it was late Friday afternoon then), and I would love to meet with her. She was very excited about the opportunity to meet an officer of the company and flattered that I would take the time to come to her house. She had said it was difficult for her to get out these days.

I hung up and formed my assault strategy. I briefed the senior-management team and previewed my plans with them. By this time, I had earned a high level of respect, not only in the home office but in the field as well. I flew to Boise on Sunday afternoon, having brought a paralegal along to help pull files and take notes. Thanks to the client, Mrs. Smith, I had copies of the fake bonds and fake statements. I knew exactly what I was looking for, though I didn't know how wide-spread the damage might be.

This registered rep, Tony Matterson, had his own office about two hours from the main office where the managing partner (Joe) sits. I knew how close the two of them were, so I waited until Sunday night to call Joe, to let him know I was in town and to brief him on the situation. I didn't want to give him too much time to alert Tony.

Joe's initial reaction was shock and disbelief. But he'd heard what kind of person I was, and if I made the trip, it must be serious. As Tony's supervisor in the field, I'm sure Joe was a little uncomfortable about how this might affect him personally. He would be in the line of fire for possible failure to supervise charges.

Joe told me he would drop what he was doing and meet me there as soon as possible. He must've driven like a bat out of hell to meet me at seven the next morning for breakfast.

I asked him a few questions about Tony. I needed to know what kind of man I was dealing with. He told me Tony was a kindhearted and intelligent person. He had a wife and three small children, lived in a wonderful home, and was well respected in the community. Tony was often on local television and hosted his own financial talk show on the radio (which I found out later had never been approved by compliance). He also had a radio program announcing all the local high-school and college football and basketball games.

He had been known to visit his clients' homes, cut their grass, do their taxes, and assist them in any way possible. Tony's family was well-connected and respected in the community too. His father was the head trustee of one of the largest churches in the area, and Tony handled all their investments.

One thing this business has taught me is the devil won't come to you with horns and fiery flames. Not all criminals carry a gun. This type of criminal wears a smile and has a personality that can light up a room. And when he walks out of the room, he will know everyone and everyone will love him.

The smart ones dress appropriately for the occasion. In New York, that means a three-piece suit. In Boise, it means rolled up sleeves and pressed jeans. They don't use guns; they use a smile and kind words that will touch your heart. They talk about your kids and the schools they attend. They are the first to volunteer at church and in the community. They're the leaders of the local Boy Scout troops and the coaches of soccer teams and little league baseball. They spend years building trust, sending out birthday cards, Christmas cards, and whatever-the-occasion cards. Mr. Perfect, president of the local Moose Club and his own tax preparation business, which included the names of everyone who was anyone in town.

It is hard going after a devil who looks like a saint and trying to put out fires when there are no flames and no one can smell the smoke but you.

When Joe and I drove up to the office, Tony was just finishing with a client. He stepped out to greet us and let us know he would be with us in a couple of minutes. His hand was shaking when he reached out to take mine, though, and he had that nervous foreboding in his eyes—that "oh shit" look. I had seen it many times before. It's the one you get when you know your entire world is about to change.

There were about ten other reps at this office, and Tony was considered the registered rep in charge. Joe briefly walked me around to introduce me. Most of them had heard me speak at the regional compliance meeting, but I was still meeting a lot of them for the first time, particularly the administrative staff.

Tony's office was completely walled-in glass, so it was easy to see when he finished with his client. She was an elderly lady who he kindly walked out to her car after their meeting. I would later discover that he took $200,000 from her that very day.

Joe and I stepped into his office as soon as they walked out. Joe told the office administrator we were not to be disturbed, just as Tony returned.

Tony gave me that bullshit smile, asked me how my trip was and whether we had plans for dinner. I didn't smile back. "Look, Tony," I said. "I'm not one to beat around the bush, so I'll cut to the chase. I believe you have been stealing money from clients, issuing fake bonds, and sending out fake statements to your clients."

He jumped up in a fit of rage. "What the fuck are you talking about? You come into my office with this ridiculous allegation and accuse me of stealing clients' money? Who the hell do you think you are? Joe, I can't believe I have to sit here and listen to this bullshit. Do you have some kind of fucking evidence of this?"

I quietly said, "You need to sit down and relax. Let me ask you this: Do you do summary statements for your clients?"

Tony said, "Yes."

"Have those summary statements been approved by compliance?"

"I regret to say, probably not."

I pulled out a copy of a statement and asked, "Is this an example of one of your statements?" I had blacked out the name of the client.

That was when the air was let out of his balloon. I asked him to explain the summary to me.

The smooth-talking salesman attitude was gone. He stuttered around an answer that made no sense at all, and finally he said, "Sometimes on the summary, I add things that the client owned but didn't purchase through me."

I asked him to give me an example.

"Like bonds, gold, and art."

I pulled out a copy of the fake bond. "Is this one of the investments you sold your clients?"

The tough-guy attitude had been reduced to the persona of a child who had just been caught with his hands in the cookie jar. He went dead silent and lowered his head down onto the desk. I think every eye in the building was glued to his office.

"These allegations are serious," I told him, "and I'm about to conduct a full investigation of your business and clients. My assistant is going through your files as we speak. Is there anything you want to tell me before I get started?"

His "I'm-smarter-than-you" reserves must have kicked in, because he lifted his head and said, "I have nothing to hide and all these allegations are untrue."

"You are hereby suspended pending further investigation. You are not to call or see any clients."

"I already have appointments scheduled."

"Joe or someone he designates will have to meet with them."

"What will you tell my clients?"

"They will be told that you are taking a leave of absence for personal reasons. For now, I need you to step out of the office while I go through your files. I will meet with your entire office to inform them of my expectations over the next couple of days."

This sort of thing is always confusing for the office personnel because they don't know me or the extent of my authority. I wanted to set up interviews with everyone in the office. Joe wasn't prepared to spend any extended time there, but he was willing to come back every day if I needed him to.

I had to move as quickly as possible to eliminate the chance of Tony destroying files or evidence. This is especially difficult to do when the rep owns the building or even pays rent for the space. I can't sit there twenty-four hours a day watching the place. And it's not advisable for me to be alone with him in his building.

Tony left the office while I spoke to everyone else there. I informed them, "I am conducting an investigation into serious allegations about Tony and his business practices." I didn't tell them what the allegations were, only that I needed their cooperation. I said, "Tony is suspended as a registered rep until further notice, and Joe will be in charge of the office. If a client calls to speak to Tony, send the calls to Joe or take a message and a phone number so someone can call them back."

Tony's assistant took it the hardest. She was a salaried employee who was paid by Tony and reported directly to him for years, and she had a ton of questions I needed to take offline. Sometimes the loyalty of a secretary can be so strong that it hinders my investigation, and I needed her to know her job wasn't in jeopardy and I needed her cooperation.

Most of the time, interviewing the assistant doesn't reveal much useful information. They usually weren't aware that a crime was being committed. They went about their days doing whatever the rep told them to do. But as always, I looked for red flags in anything Tony's assistant said or did, and in this case, she told me that Tony liked to handle a lot of his own correspondence with certain clients. Red flag. He would send clients letters and cards on his own—she knew this because when she did the mail, there always seemed to be a lot of letters to people who she wasn't asked to send things to.

To calm her fears, I let her know that for now the company would pick up her salary and I would let her know if something were to change that might affect her position.

I had my assistant Julie, download all the information from Tony's office computer. As I was going through Tony's desk, I found his operating checkbook in his desk drawer and discovered something interesting and a little unusual. Usually, an operating checkbook contains checks made out to the landlord, the electric company, the printer company, the phone company, and similar administrative essentials—bills owed for the operation and upkeep of the office. While I found those, I also discovered checks made out to individuals. This was another red flag. So, I donned my *CSI* hat again.

As a compliance officer, I have to spot anything that looks out of place. I have to notice when things are missing. And I have to pay attention to things that just don't seem to fit. Why are so many checks made out to individuals? Who were these people? Some checks went to the same individuals every month, some appeared to be quarterly. I thought these might be dividend or interest payments to people he had sold fake bonds to.

I had Julie make copies of all those checks. Then I asked her to pull the files on the names. There were no files matching them, so I had Julie send the names to the home office to see if they matched any names in our database. They still didn't. I needed to know who these people were, so I did it the old-fashioned way: I went to the white pages.

I know. But this was a small town, and believe it or not, in some towns they still produce a local residential phone book.

A Teaching Moment

There are many types of individual bonds. I won't go into all of them, but generally, bonds pay interest on a quarterly basis. You cannot reinvest this interest into the same bond; you would have to put it into another bond or some other bond-like instrument. If you were being paid the interest directly, the checks would most likely come from a paying agent of the bond. This is usually a large banking institution, not a registered rep. There should never be a time when you receive personal checks from a registered rep.

Back to the White Pages

To my surprise, I found quite a few of the names in the white pages. I called a few and introduced myself as the chief compliance officer and regulatory supervisor over Tony Matterson. I told them the company often reviews our registered reps and the kinds of investments they were recommending to our clients. I said if it was possible, I would like to meet with them about their investments and find out how they felt about working with Tony. I would be happy to meet them at their home or at Tony's office. They were very gracious and happy to meet an officer of the company. Some said they welcomed the opportunity to tell the company how happy they were with Tony. Some were skeptical but wouldn't mind coming into the office to meet me. So Julie and I started scheduling appointments, some in the office and some at the clients' homes.

CHAPTER 13

Mrs. Smith

AFTER A FEW calls, it was time to visit Mrs. Smith, the lady who had contacted the home office to ask about her tax-free bond. I took Julie with me. Though Julie didn't understand why, I asked her to take the lead in knocking at the door and making the opening statement about who we were. I think she got it when she saw Mrs. Smith's first reaction to seeing a black guy she didn't know at her front door. I've been around long enough to know it's just the reality of things.

Mrs. Smith was a very nice lady in her eighties. I made the formal introductions once we entered the house, and both Julie and I handed her our business cards. Mrs. Smith was perceptive and immediately asked why Julie's card differed from mine.

It's sometimes difficult for people to understand, but when these situations arise, they often bring three different entities into play, the first being the Tony Matterson Financial Company. Because our reps are independent agents, they have their own local business names. The second, the name on Julie's card, was her employer, the parent company. And the third, the broker-dealer's name, which was a separate registered company, wholly owned by the parent company.

I was a dual employee of both the parent company and the broker-dealer, which by law, must be a separate stand-alone entity.

It's confusing, I know, and it's not a good thing when the client, who doesn't really know you, has an instant reason for doubt. But Mrs. Smith grew more comfortable as our conversation progressed, and she understood the connection between the companies. She was a retired schoolteacher, and Tony had once been her student.

She'd known him from the time he was a baby; in fact, she'd known his father all her life. She was very close to his family. She attended the same church as they did, and she had worked with Tony for as long as he had been in the business. She told me she was very proud of Tony and trusted him with all her finances. He even did her taxes, and he was the trustee of her trust account down at the bank (which, by the way, violated our policy).

A Teaching Moment

Never put all your eggs in one basket. You've probably heard that maxim a thousand times. Diversify not only your investments but who you do business with. You need a system that allows for checks and balances to occur naturally; your investment adviser should not be the person who does your taxes and that person should be different from the person you do your banking with.

Back to Mrs. Smith

She told me Tony knew the combination to her safe and would handle anything that needed to be done. Tony was the one who put in her sprinkler system and cut her grass. She loved him and trusted him like a son.

With every heartfelt compliment, my job was getting more difficult. I looked over at Julie and her eyes had already started to fill with tears.

Mrs. Smith said, "I'm very happy with my investments, in particular the tax-free bond that Tony sold me. I'm thankful and pleased to get a check from him every month for the interest." That explained why her name had been in the checkbook I found. He had to keep up the charade of paying people who wanted their income.

I asked her if she knew anyone else who had invested in these bonds. She was pleased to give me the names of several people, including the church. She said they were all satisfied with the bonds.

Now came the hard part. How do I tell a person who doesn't know me or my company from Adam that someone she loves, trusts, and has known all his life is a thief? That the bonds she's so happy about are fake and the only reason she gets checks every month is because Tony is stealing the money from someone else to pay her.

Unlike other victims of these types of crimes, Mrs. Smith would be heartbroken long before she might be grateful I was there looking out for her.

I knew that once I finished this conversation, whether or not Mrs. Smith believed me, the floodgates would open and all hell would break loose. There would be no turning back. She would be on the phone with everyone she could reach to tell her story; maybe even with the police, saying I was trying to con her and take her bonds.

The important thing was to make her as comfortable as possible. To speak from the heart and not from some script. To convince her I was there to help her and take care of her. I represented a company that cared about her and our clients. Somehow, I had to get her to trust someone she didn't know and to shatter her trust in someone she had known all his life. I started by telling her about myself and what I do.

"Mrs. Smith, I am the chief compliance officer of a very large company in Minnesota. I am responsible for the regulatory supervision of approximately three thousand registered reps from all over the country. My staff and I handle all complaints, concerns, investigations, and audits for the company. I also go after bad reps when they take advantage of people: I've fired dozens of bad reps, and I've helped prosecute and put more than twenty people in jail during my career. The reason I'm telling you all this is because what I'm about to tell you will be very hard to believe and very upsetting.

"First, let me ask Julie to pull up information about the bond market on her laptop. I want to show you the kind of interest rates a U.S. Government tax-free bond is paying these days."

We looked up a bond, and I pointed out the numbers to her. "As you can see, the interest rate for a tax-free bond is only 2%. Your bond is paying 9%, which is incredibly high by comparison. So, let's look up your bond …"

Julie typed the description and title of the bond into the computer, and it said "No match."

Then we typed in the CUSIP number and it said "No match."

A bewildered expression came over Mrs. Smith's face. "Why is my bond not coming up?"

"Remember when I first spoke to you on the phone, and I kept asking you to read off the CUSIP number to me?"

"Yes."

"I knew that the last three digits of a CUSIP number for a bond should be letters, not numbers. That's why I asked you to fax me a copy, so I could verify it myself. That's also why I brought copies of authentic government bonds, so you could see for yourself what they look like, and it's why I'm having Julie key them up on the computer. I've also brought copies of actual client statements so you can see what they look like."

Then I finally said, "Mrs. Smith, this bond you have is a fake. This statement you have is also a fake. We in the corporate office have no record in our system of you or any investment for you. We do not know you as a client."

Her eyes fill with tears, and she didn't stop crying for ten minutes. Neither did Julie.

"Mrs. Smith, the reason I came here today was to deliver this news to you personally. But more importantly, I came here to let you know my company and I care about you, and I'm here to make this right. Please have no fear; we will make sure that all your money is returned to you, and we will make you whole."

Mrs. Smith was still looking for a way to believe in Tony. She asked me, "Could this be accidental?" At first, I wasn't sure what she meant by that. Then she continued, "Did Tony know the bonds were fake?"

Most people have never seen a real bond or stock certificate.

Possibly, she thought or hoped that Tony had been swindled into thinking he had bought real bonds and unknowingly passed them on to her.

"No, Mrs. Smith," I said. "He knew what he was doing. He was printing these bonds and your statements himself. The mistake Tony made was that he didn't know how the CUSIP system works. He only knew a CUSIP number was nine digits and should be on the certificate but he didn't know the last three digits for bonds are letters, not numbers. If it weren't deliberate, he would have sent your paperwork into the home office for processing. But in order to get away with the fraud, he would have to hide it from you and from us."

"But why? Why would he do this?" she asked.

"I don't know, Mrs. Smith. He's been very uncooperative with me so far. I know this is a lot for you to take in—is there anyone you could call to be with you?"

"I'll be fine," she said. "How can I verify what you have been telling me?"

"You can call the headquarters and anyone there will verify who I am. You can also come down to Tony's office, I will be there all week and anyone there can verify who I am and what I do."

She told me she was living on the monthly checks Tony was sending her and that she depended on them. I told her it would take some time to resolve all this, but that I would do my best to take care of her.

"You have my number, please feel free to call me anytime, day or night."

She finally asked, "What will happen to Tony?"

"I fired Tony this morning. I made it clear that he can no longer work with clients or use our computer system to advise clients. He may be in the office from time to time to collect personal items or regarding his tax business, because I don't have authority over those things. These are federal crimes, and once I finish my investigation, I will meet with the Assistant Attorney General's office. The case will be assigned to the FBI, and sometime after that, they will arrest Tony and he will go to jail."

The floodgate of tears opened up again, and I asked if she was all right. She said, "Oh my God, he invested all the church's money in those bonds."

I asked for the name of a contact at the church, she told me, "It's Tony's father … Can I talk to Tony?"

"I don't know what Tony will tell you. I've told him he isn't allowed to talk to clients. I'm sure he'll verify who I am. But I don't know what else he might say. I advise against it, but I understand if you feel you must do that."

I asked Mrs. Smith to gather up as much information as she could and bring it to Tony's office tomorrow, where one of the office assistants would make copies of everything.

Mrs. Smith was devastated because all the money she had saved and all the money her deceased husband left her had been entrusted to Tony. She didn't know how she would make it. She didn't know how someone she trusted and loved so much, someone who had keys to her house and could come and go as he pleased, could both help her with everything and steal everything she needed.

When you find out that a fast-talking salesman has taken advantage of you, you simply get mad. But when it's someone you love and trust, someone who comes to your house every day smiling and pretending to care about you, while they are actually embezzling your last dime—well it just breaks your heart, in a way that getting mad could never compare to.

I talk to reps all the time, and they tell me stories that the hardest, but most satisfying, part of their job is the moment when they get to deliver the proceeds of a life-insurance policy.

But at least in those cases, you leave the beneficiary with a check. It will never replace the person they lost, but it can ease the pressure and stress of some future obligations.

The life-insurance side of the company hangs their hat on the vision that "we have a promise to pay" in the event of a personal tragedy. But people like Mrs. Smith didn't have a death related to an insurance policy. There was no promise to pay, just my promise to do the right thing. We had failed to protect Mrs. Smith, but I would not fail to take care of her.

What I told Mrs. Smith came from the heart, not our attorneys or senior management trying to protect their own asses. No one trains you to talk from the heart. You either do or you don't. You are either real or you're not, and people can tell. I only know one way to be and that's real. And Mrs. Smith knew it.

Julie gave Mrs. Smith a hug as we said goodbye. It's a lot easier confronting a criminal than breaking the heart of an innocent victim. Neither Julie nor myself was prepared for such an emotional roller-coaster ride. As soon as we got in the car, Julie asked why I didn't have Mrs. Smith sign the release forms.

Of course, the attorneys always stick their hands in the mix. They are the ones holding the purse strings, so I had to listen. They wanted me to have each client sign a form acknowledging the "misappropriation" of the funds, stating they were unaware the bonds were fake and that they had a reasonable expectation of an appropriate investment.

They would also agree not to sue us once we paid them back their principal with the appropriate return on their investment. Somehow, I had to work that into the mix. Speak from the heart but protect the pocketbook. I get that. Just like the military, I had my orders, and I wasn't in charge.

I told Julie that I didn't feel this was the right time but I would have her sign them when she came into the office.

There's another aspect of this investigation that gets a little complicated. I had to be reasonably sure that these people truly were or thought they were clients of ours—not someone working with Tony just to get paid. Keep in mind that he stood up at the compliance meeting and asked what would happen if we discovered someone was stealing from a client. Me and my big mouth told him the clients would get all their money back. In other words, I now had to make sure these were legitimate cases.

CHAPTER 14

The Unexpected

NEXT ON THE list were Mr. and Mrs. Larson. They weren't far, but I took my time so that Julie could pull herself together.

The Larsons seemed pleasant when we introduced ourselves. The conversation started off pretty much the same as with Mrs. Smith. Mr. Larson showed me their statement and copies of the bonds. We showed them the comparisons on the laptop. But something didn't feel right. As our conversation went on, Mrs. Larson was quite concerned, and we could tell she was physically upset, but Mr. Larson seemed standoffish and cold.

Then I explained that the bonds were fake. Our company was there to look after them and make sure they got their money back, but I needed them to sign the document confirming and acknowledging the theft. Mr. Larson flew into a fit of fury. He was a big guy, and Julie looked nervous as he stood up and started yelling and cussing me out, as if I was the one who had stolen his money.

"Who the fuck do you think you are, coming around here making these wild accusations about my nephew?"

Oops. I didn't know that part.

Mrs. Larson tried to calm him down, but it was too late. He was out of control.

"I know a bit about this business!" he shouted. "And it's your fucking job to supervise Tony. It's your fault this shit happened, and you are totally responsible for it! I'm not going to sign your fucking document! You get the hell out of my house before I throw you out!"

Well, I know when to talk and when to shut up. It was time to shut up and exit.

Mrs. Larson said, "You should leave now," and she didn't have to tell me twice.

Mr. Larson was still screaming. "Got damn it, I told you to get the hell out of my house!" He ran back into the bedroom for something, and I was not waiting to find out what. This was not the time to pull that tough Eastside of Detroit attitude out of my hat. Besides, Julie was crying and shaking so bad that I was concerned about her safety. So we made a quick exit.

"Well, that could have gone better," I said.

Julie tried to smile, but she was still shaking like a leaf. I had one more appointment that day, so I needed her to pull it together.

She asked me, "How can you handle this so calmly? That was the worst thing I've ever experienced."

"Things never go the way you plan. Someone has to keep a level head, or it can get dangerous. This is what I do. I may not know what's coming next, but I know God put me in this job, and He will watch over me. Besides, I've seen a lot worse on the East Side of Detroit."

Then she smiled.

Our last appointment for the day was with Mr. and Mrs. Jackson. They were a nice elderly couple. Our conversation started off like the previous two, and the Jacksons were very happy to show me their paperwork and copies of their bonds. Unlike the Larsons, they took the news about Tony and the fake bonds very well.

I was surprised at how smoothly this all went. Mrs. Jackson said in a very calm voice, "This is very disturbing news, but we're very well off and have other means of taking care of ourselves."

I said, "Even though that may be the case, it's my job to make sure you get all your money back; and there must be consequences for Tony and his actions. I do need you to sign these documents, so I can pursue action against Tony. We can't allow him the opportunity to take advantage of you or others who may not be so fortunate."

Mrs. Jackson said, "We're very appreciative and grateful for the information you've given us but we can't sign the document. We're going to put this in God's hands, and He will take care of us."

"It's already in God's hands. That's why He sent me here—to take care of it and to take care of you. I grew up in a very poor part of Detroit," I told them. "Most of my friends are dead, on drugs, or in jail. Fifteen years ago, God put me on a different path. He brought me out of Detroit and gave me this job, and He did that for one reason and one reason only: to protect people like you and Mr. Jackson. I'm here because the matter is already in God's hands."

She looked at me and started to cry. I couldn't stop her tears or my own. Then she said, "I believe God did send you here," and she signed the document.

This was a tough day and only the beginning of many more tough conversations to come. I had never broken down in front of a client or co-worker before. It was new territory for me and I knew I needed God's strength to see me through it.

It was time to call it a day. Time to go back to the office and collect as much data as I could. I had the managing partner and Tony's assistant boxing up files for me while I was gone, and they'd done a great job. I sent most of it by Federal Express to the home office for my team to conduct a thorough analysis.

Tony came into the office while I was there to ask when he could get back into his office. He tried to insist forcefully that some files were personal and had nothing to do with the investment business.

I told him, "You should have read the annual questionnaire you signed, acknowledging that all files in a registered office and of a registered rep would be subject to inspection at any time by a regulator or a compliance officer."

Most registered reps seem to think they're much smarter than home-office people. They must have it in their minds that if home-office people were smarter, they'd be out selling and making more money. But I'm used to this arrogance and don't pay any attention to it. Tony wanted to get back into his office, but I was in no hurry to let that happen.

But I wasn't so naïve as to think that he wouldn't be there in the middle of the night going through things, so I needed to get as much as I could as soon as I could.

He was shocked when he saw all the boxes I had prepared to be shipped out. He gave the usual rep speech about how I had no right to do this or that. It went in one ear and out the other. He told me that he needed to pay some bills and asked if he could at least have his checkbook from his desk.

I smiled and said of course. I asked him again, "Is there anything you want to tell me?"

"Like what?" he answered.

"Like how many clients you sold those fake bonds to and why you did it?"

"I haven't sold anybody any fake bonds!"

"It would be much better for you if you told me now. But it really doesn't matter. I'll find out—with or without your help."

He apparently had no idea that I had already met with some clients. And I'm sure he didn't know that the only reason I gave him the checkbook was that I had already copied everything in it and downloaded everything from his computer. This wasn't my first rodeo.

So, he took the checkbook and left. I would later find out that this wasn't his first rodeo either.

The next morning, I was at the office bright and early. Another rep, Beth, came in while I was going through some paperwork. "May I speak with you?" she asked.

"Yes, come in."

"Is it true?" she asked.

"Is what true?"

"Has Tony been selling fake bonds and stealing money from clients?"

"Where did you hear that?"

"Word's all over town."

"Yes, it's true."

She gasped. "Oh my God, What about Ziggy?"

"Who's Ziggy?"

"Tony's partner. They often wrote business together and some-times handle each other's clients if one of them is on vacation or something."

"Ziggy is not on my list of registered reps."

"No, he wouldn't be. He works for another broker-dealer," she explained.

My case had just become more complicated. In order for Tony to split commissions with other reps, he needed written permission from me, and I knew I hadn't given that permission to anyone.

Beth started crying, and I didn't know why. "What's wrong?" I asked.

"Tony and I … we're close friends. He was the one who brought me into the business." Then she said something that shocked the hell out of me. "My husband and I bought some of those bonds from Tony a few years earlier, before I became a registered rep."

"Damn." I'm not sure if I said that out loud or to myself. Either way, I couldn't believe what I was hearing. "You're a registered rep, and you didn't know you were sold fake bonds? What about your statements? You had to know they weren't legitimate. You know what a statement looks like, don't you? Are you fucking kidding me?"

By then, she was crying so hard that I needed to tone down my sarcasm. Still, I was beside myself in disbelief.

"I never had any reason to doubt them or even pay close attention to them."

This was the dumbest shit I'd ever heard! I said that in my mind, of course, not to her. She felt bad enough knowing that she'd been duped by a (so-called) close friend and coworker.

I started thinking though. This woman worked with Tony every day. How long did he think he could get away with this? How long did he think it would be before she found out what real bonds looked like? Maybe their friendship went to another level. Maybe he was keeping her so close that she didn't want to see. It was just a thought.

I told her to bring me copies of everything she had. I also wanted a written statement from her about the entire process of Tony selling her the bonds. "I have to be honest though," I said. "I'm not sure how they're going to treat your case. They look at you as a professional and have higher expectations regarding what you know or should have known. But I'll present it and see what happens."

What her story told me was that Tony had been doing this for a while. There was no telling how deep or wide this problem went.

Later that day, I was sitting in Tony's office on the phone. Through the glass, I saw two guys standing over Tony, where he was sitting at a desk in the front. At first glance, I thought one of them was choking him. Maybe that was just wishful thinking. As it turned out, they were laying hands on him and praying.

One guy I recognized as Tony's uncle, the one that threw us out of his house. The other turned out to be his father, who was my next scheduled meeting of the day. I can only imagine how that conversation must have gone the night before. "Hey Dad, I stole a few million dollars from clients. As well as Uncle Lewis and Aunt Ruth's money. Oh, and did I mention, all the church's money too. Sorry..."

Mr. Matterson Sr. came over to the office and asked to speak to me. He told me that his son had told him everything. I needed to hear what he meant by "everything," though, so I asked him, "Would you mind telling me what your son has told you? He hasn't been very cooperative with me."

Mr. Matterson Sr. said, "I apologize for that, but I think it'd be better if it came from him. I would also like to apologize for what my son has done and for the behavior of my brother-in-law. I understand that meeting didn't go well. He was quite upset, and from what I hear, he overreacted. I assure you that my son's cooperation will be forthcoming and that my brother-in-law will sign any document you want."

"Thank you," I said. "But let's talk about your situation. I understand that you represent the church. Did the church invest in these bonds?"

"Yes."

"How much did they invest?"

"$500,000."

"Well, Mr. Matterson, as you're already aware, I'm afraid those bonds are fakes. I'll need supporting documentation from you regarding your meeting with Tony, as it relates to the investment. I'll also need paperwork from the church authorizing you as their representative. At that time, I'll have some documents for you to sign, and then we can begin the process of getting the church's money back."

"Can I speak to you as a father for a moment?"

I nodded. "Of course."

"What's going to happen to my son?"

"Yesterday, I fired him as a registered representative of this company and suspended his securities and insurance licenses. I've alerted the state and federal authorities. Once I finish my investigation, I'll present it to the Assistant U.S. Attorney General's office and they'll assign the case to the FBI. They'll arrest Tony. He'll most likely serve six to eight years in prison."

As strong as he appeared to be, he was not able to hold back the tears of a loving father. With that, he thanked me for my time, apologized again for his son, and left.

If only Tony had the integrity and strength of his father, I mused.

The office was buzzing with activity. The phones were ringing off the hook, and people were coming out of the woodwork asking questions and looking for help. One unfortunate consequence of these situations is that every client of every rep in the office is concerned about their own accounts. The news was traveling fast, and reporters were also calling now and hanging around the doors of the office.

My team back in the home office was busy doing a forensic analysis of each client's case, and once again circling the wagons to prepare for regulatory action and possible client lawsuits.

Among the boxes I sent them, they came across something interesting and quite damaging for the company. It turns out Tony had been caught doing something similar about five years before I arrived. He had sold a client a promissory note guaranteeing a high interest rate.

Bonds and promissory notes are basically the same thing. According to the files, this had come to light as a result of a complaint from a client. But apparently, the only consequence was that Tony had to pay back the client's money, and he received a warning letter which he signed with a promise not to do it again. They never even checked to see if other clients had been sold a promissory note. Nor did they put him under heightened supervision to make sure he wouldn't do it again. Minnesota nice …

Maybe that was why he walked around with such an arrogant attitude. This wasn't his first rodeo: he had been here before. He most likely thought he would never be caught, or that if he was, a slap on the wrist would be all he got—he could use his killer smile, charming personality, and smooth salesmanship to finesse his way out of anything more.

But there was a new sheriff in town, and I didn't give a damn about his salesmanship. I won't bore you with the details of all the victims I met with. In total, it came to twenty-eight clients and $8,000,000.

To be precise, there were actually twenty-nine victims. One, Mr. Hann, told me he would handle his own situation, including the return of his money.

I didn't understand at first, but I later learned that he took a shotgun over to Tony's house and was able to negotiate the return of all his money right on the spot. I would have loved to be a fly on the wall during that conversation! I tried to get my boss to let me hire Mr. Hann, but he didn't think he was a good fit. Oh well.

The next time I saw Tony, he was being marched into the courtroom in an orange jumpsuit with chains around his ankles. He had lost that killer smile and his arrogant attitude.

I spoke at the sentencing hearing, representing the company as a victim. When asked, I told the court, "These crimes cannot go unpunished. I speak in front of thousands of reps every year and tell them the stories of how people screwed up. Reps are in a position of trust. They work in an industry built on trust. They need to know that if a registered rep takes advantage of that trust, there are serious consequences. There is a high standard of integrity for the things we do. Elderly people are easy prey. The punishment for their abuse should be twice what it is for other people. People come to you for advice—whether good or bad: they understand that you're not always right. But it is unacceptable to take advantage of these people just because you can.

"If you do the crime, you will do the time, I tell reps. And that time should be meaningful. I have to be able to tell the reps that crimes they commit against seniors and unsuspecting people are just as serious as using a gun to hold up a liquor store, and it will get you just as meaningful an amount of time in prison."

Tony pleaded guilty to all charges and was sentenced to six years in prison. Every one of his clients got their money back, and not one of them sued us. I still get Christmas cards from some of them.

CHAPTER 15

True Confessions

THEY SAY CONFESSION is good for the soul. I believe that with all my heart. I rarely hear many confessions in my job, at least not before I've backed someone into a corner with so much evidence they have no choice but to confess. But there were two exceptions.

The first started when a rep insisted on speaking with me one day. A number of people tried to help him, but he wouldn't have it. He would only speak to me and me only. I knew this rep; we'd met several times over the years. I was pretty busy at the time he called, but I eventually got back with him.

I had been telling reps for years that if they had a problem or foresaw one, they should call me first and not try to resolve it themselves. Be careful what you ask for. The first thing he said to me was, "You might get a call from the police department because I got caught doing something I shouldn't have. Have you got a call yet?"

"No, I haven't. Do you want to tell me what you did?"

"I'm embarrassed to admit this," he said, "but you're always telling reps they should come to you first with a problem." Well, at least I knew they were listening to me.

He continued, "I trust you and I couldn't tell anyone else. Don't worry, I didn't steal anything or take advantage of anyone."

I had been holding my breath, so at least now I could breathe.

Then he said, "Look, I don't have a very good reason why I did this and even worse where I did it. But I did, so anyway, I was driving alone in my car, and I stopped at a stop sign and started masturbating."

There was a very long pause, and I knew I wasn't going to say anything. I mean, did he really say, masturbating?

"The thing is," he said, "I have a convertible, and the top was down. I must have been concentrating on what I was doing because I didn't notice this lady that pulled up right beside me until she started yelling and screaming at me. She told me she had taken down my license-plate number and was going straight to the police to report me.

"So, while I'm embarrassed about what I did, I'm more scared about what the police might do."

I was at a loss for words. I wasn't at all prepared for this, and I was a little unsure how to even react. I stayed calm but didn't ask why he'd done it. I guess the damnedest things can pop into your head—not to mention your hand—while you're driving. I guess.

"Well, I understand now why you only wanted to speak to me," I said. "I'll do my best to make sure it stays between us. I haven't got a call yet. And it's likely the lady was just making a threat and didn't actually go to the police. Either way, I'll make sure that if any calls come in, they come directly to me, and I'll handle it personally."

"Thank you, I appreciate that."

When I hung the phone up, I was wondering what was he thinking that caused such an urgency in his mind to do that, right then, right there. Anyway, the police never called and I never officially documented his call. I guess if there was a lesson to be learned from this, it would be to keep both hands on the wheel at all times while driving.

The second confession wasn't nearly as provocative as the first, but at least it was a little more in line with what I'm used to! For years I'd been going around saying, "No rep has ever called me and said 'I stole money from a client.'"

Never say never.

The call came in like any other call: "I'd like to speak to the chief compliance officer. I'm a registered rep from the Bethesda office."

"How can I help you?" I asked him.

"I'm calling to let you know you're about to receive a complaint from one of my clients. The complaint will say I stole $300,000 from their account. And it's true. But you should know the client is my father."

All I could say was, "Are you serious?"

He said, "Yes, I am."

"How did this happen?"

The rep told me the story. "Every time I would ask my father for a loan he would always say no. So, I've been withdrawing small amounts from his account for the last few years. He's been constantly asking me for statements, and I've been giving him all kinds of excuses. So the other day, he got so upset that he stormed into my office, demanding copies of his statements. I had to finally break down and tell him everything."

"How were you able to order checks out without causing any red flags?" I asked him.

"I've been ordering checks from his account in his name so that no red flags popped up—the checks were made out to my father and sent to his home address. I'd then go over to the house and retrieve them. Cashing them was no problem because I have the same name as my father."

Yeah, that could work, I thought.

"I spoke to my father last night, so now he knows. Not surprisingly, he threw a fit. I told him I could pay him back in small amounts over time, but he wouldn't hear of it. He said I have to face the consequences like anyone else who steals money. So he'll be sending you the complaint soon. You should also know, although I know you'll check anyway, I didn't do this to any other clients. I needed the money and he wouldn't lend it to me. So I took it."

Needless to say, I was stunned. I told him I'd need everything he just told me in writing. I would also check his other clients and I would need all his files. He agreed to FedEx everything to me. The rep kept his word and sent me everything. His father kept his word also and sent in the complaint about his son and followed through with the prosecution of his son, who was fired, booted out of the industry, and went to prison for five years.

CHAPTER **16**

"I Didn't Steal from Clients"

YOU MAY REMEMBER me saying how registered reps need approval from compliance to be paid for any activity outside their duties as a rep. Here's why I'm reminding you: it was a Monday morning when one of my coworkers walked into my office and asked me if I'd read an article about Kris, one of our reps, in the Sunday's paper. I said no, and he handed it to me.

According to the article, Kris had been arrested for stealing $45,000 from the treasury of the local Republican Party, while he was serving as treasurer. Apparently, he both stole the money and repaid it before the new treasurer discovered it, and because he had repaid it, he pleaded guilty to a lesser charge and had to serve time doing community service.

First off, Kris never had approval from me to be the treasurer for the Republican Party. Second, he never told us about the charges or the conviction, which violates our policies and his responsibility to report. Of course, I couldn't just go by what I read in the paper; I had to confirm it. But it would take a while to get all the court documents, so I called the rep to see what he was willing to share with me.

Surprisingly, he told me everything. But his next comment surprised me even more.

"Why do you ask? This has nothing to do with my job as a registered rep."

"You were found guilty of stealing $45,000 from the treasury of the Republican Party, which in itself violates our Code of Ethics policy," I said. "Plus you didn't get approval from us to even be the treasurer. So, I'm asking to confirm if it's true. And if it is true, to terminate you for, 1. not getting approval before you took the job as treasurer, and 2. violating the Code of Ethics policy, which states that if you're charged with a financial crime and plead guilty to a lesser crime, even if it's outside your job as a registered rep, you are disqualified from working in a broker-dealer."

His last words were, "How can you fire me? Yes, I stole the money, but it wasn't from a client and I paid it back." His logic was simple but flawed. He just didn't get that the only way for anyone to have trust in the industry was *complete* honesty—whoever you stole from.

CHAPTER **17**

A Proud Moment

I WAS WALKING through the airport when I heard someone call my name. I turned around and was shocked to see an old friend from high school, Cory Hunter. We sat down and took a few minutes to catch up, and when it was time to leave, we exchanged business cards. When he read mine, he said, "Oh shit? You're a senior vice president."

"Yes."

He said, "You've got to come back to the old school and speak to the graduating class. We've had our share of sports figures, and a few singers too, but no one has ever come back to speak with the students."

I was flattered and honored, but puzzled. "But I'm just a person who has a good job. I'm no celebrity or anything."

"Trust me, Loyall, you're just what we need."

So I said, "Of course I'll come. Just send me the info."

With that, we both ran to catch our planes.

Later that week, I was having coffee with my boss when I told him I would be speaking at my old high school. He was as proud of me as I was proud to do it, and he said the company would happily pay for the trip. I really wasn't expecting that but I was grateful.

The company had an office in Lansing that I visited a few times a year, but I hadn't been back to Detroit much, and mostly just for funerals and such. Kettering Senior High School was one of the worst schools on the East Side of Detroit. Or maybe, I should say, it was a good school in one of the worst areas on the East Side. I think they had metal detectors on the doors before some airports had them. Either way, it was right in the middle of the hood.

My cousin once told me, "If you ever have to go to prison, make sure they send you to Jackson, because you'll know half the people there; they're from Kettering and will take care of you!" While I appreciated the advice, going to jail was not on my bucket list.

The students were tough. And unless you were Magic Johnson or some singer from Motown, you wouldn't gain much respect there. But Cory was right: no one ever returned once they got out. So, I had nothing to lose. All I had to do was reach one person, and it would be worthwhile.

Just as I started to speak, the first question jumped out at me loud and clear: "So, why are you here talking to us? Where are you from?"

"I live in Minnesota but I'm from Detroit."

"Just because you from Detroit, don't mean you know the hood," someone said.

"No, it doesn't. But I grew up on the corner of Holcomb and Mack."

The room fell dead silent. Then I heard someone say, "That's the real hood."

"Yes, it is."

Then I gave them my street resume. I graduated from Kettering, did four years in the Navy, worked on the line at Ford Motor Company, and attended Christ Baptist Church. My grandfather was Coleman Young's[2] cousin and ran numbers out of Janie's Restaurant on Mack and Van Dyke. I had a son who was shot and killed a few blocks from here. There's a mural painted on this garage in his honor. It says "Rest in Peace, Loyall."

"Shit, I knew him!" someone shouted out.

Now I had their attention. "I ran those streets," I told them. "But I

---

2   Coleman Young helped found the National Negro Labor Council in 1951 was Detroit's first African American mayor, serving twenty years, 1974–1994.

didn't let the streets run me." Then I gave them my new and improved resume. The one God had written for me. I told them how God had kicked my chair and woken me up. All I had to do was listen, stay focused on what was right, and step out on faith.

"I'm not here to promise you anything," I said. "I'm here just to tell you what happened to me. If you want to change something, don't sit around waiting for it to change. Change it. It may not be easy, but it's not as hard as the streets."

As it turned out, I was speaking to one of Kettering's last graduating classes. The school was shut down and has been sitting closed for over fifteen years.

God must have been kicking my chair again at just the right time.

CHAPTER 18

The Colonel

I ONCE SAW the president of the company chitchatting with an officer of the U.S. Airforce. As I walked by, Bob called me over to introduce me: "I want you to meet Colonel John Brown." He had about seven inches of medals on his chest. "John, this is Loyall Wilson, our chief compliance officer."

The first thing out of his mouth was, "I'm the most compliant person you'll ever meet. I have a great deal of respect for compliance, and you'll have no concerns from me or the people that work for me."

I said, "Nice to meet you, sir," but I was thinking: same comments, different rep. We get these "compliance quotes" all the time: "It's nice to meet you, but I hope we don't have to meet again." "It's nice to meet you, but I hope you have no reason to remember my name." "I am the most compliant person you will ever meet."

Col. Brown had just retired from the Air Force.

"While I don't know a lot about the investment business," he said, "I'm looking forward to the opportunity to serve people as I served my country."

Wow, words to live by.

"I know what following rules and regulations are all about, and how important they are."

It was a couple of years before I heard his name again. When I did, he didn't appear to be serving his country or his clients; he appeared to be serving himself.

By this time, my team had really developed into experts in the field of compliance. I was no longer doing audits myself, but I was still running most of the investigations. Whenever anyone on the team had concerns, they would bring them to our morning meeting to give all the other members of our team an opportunity to discuss and learn from each other. Then once a month, I would give that same opportunity to leaders in other areas of the company, for them to share with their teams. It was important to me that these learning opportunities found their way into every part of the company. That way, the eyes of compliance would not be limited to the compliance team but would be stretched throughout the organization.

I had also developed a thorough system of checks and balances. If one person collected money, someone else would count it, and a third person would periodically check that count. Then I would review to verify they completed all steps.

Here's how I know the system works. During one audit, we discovered that a client of Colonel Brown's had signed a letter of authorization for $25,000 to be withdrawn from his account. It was then to be deposited in a bank account in the name of the Jackson High School Reunion.

Anytime a client signs a withdrawal form to have money transferred into an account in a name other than the client's own, I put an extra step in place to protect the client. In this case, the client's signature had to be stamped with one of our signature-guarantee stamps.

A Teaching Moment

A medallion signature-guarantee stamp is authorized by the industry specifically for documents involving the transfer of money and securities through banks and other financial institutions. It shares some similarities to a notary stamp. It is a system in which a few selected people have the power to guarantee the authenticity of a signature.

Back to the Story

The person signing the document had to be in the presence of the person with the stamp. Each office that was authorized to have a stamp had to keep a record of when it was used for each signature. Although the letter of authorization in question had the appropriate stamp on it, the office log showed no such entry. That was my check and balance system, telling me something was wrong.

Upon further review, the auditor discovered there had been several withdrawals from this account, and the signatures were in exactly the same spot on each letter. Even the spacing of the signature and the position of the stamp were identical. This observation led the auditor to believe we were looking at photocopies of a single letter of authorization that had been used several times for different amounts. In other words, a forged document.

When the auditor brought the information to my attention, I confirmed her findings and opened an official investigation. I first looked to see if this was happening with any other clients, of the colonel's. That turned up negative, which was a good thing.

Then I moved on to the bank. When a registered rep was first hired, I had them sign a form allowing us to review their bank statements whenever I saw fit. Most reps don't think about this or even remember it, plus I usually only do it when I have concerns. In this case, the bank account wasn't in the name of the rep, but in the name of the Jackson High School Reunion. Maybe he thought the different name would throw me off, or I wouldn't comprehensively do my homework. I'm not sure. But I found out that the authorized signers on the account were the colonel and his wife. Over a period of about two years, they had transferred almost $500,000 from the client's account into this bank account. That was going to be one hell of a reunion party.

I paid the office a surprise visit. I wanted to get a little history on the person who had the authority to use the stamp and on the colonel, who, by the way, was not located in the same branch as the managing partner.

Robert, the managing partner, was quite nervous when he saw me walk in. The first thing he said was, "This can't be good."

"It's not," I said. "Can we talk in your office?"

I told Robert how I had concerns about the proper use of the signature-guarantee stamp. He had all kinds of questions for me, but I wasn't ready to answer them. Sometimes, I have to weed out who is and who is not involved in a particular situation. In this office, the office manager, Debra, who was also Robert's secretary, was the keeper of the stamp.

He asked me, "Is Debra in trouble?"

"I'm not sure yet, but I need to speak with her. Could you have her come in please?"

Robert had her come in and made the introductions.

"Debra, as the keeper of the signature-guarantee stamp, I need to ask you a few questions. I have a copy of a Letter of Authorization that was signature guaranteed using your stamp, but there was no corresponding entry in the log. Can you help me understand why?"

She examined the letter and a sense of ease came over her face. "I recognize this client," she said. "This was done for Mr. Cisco. He's a high-profile client of Colonel Brown, who travels a lot. Robert said it was ok to let the colonel take the stamp with him because he can't meet the client very often, and Mr. Cisco can never find the time to come into the main branch."

Robert chimed in to confirm that he had given Debra permission to do that. Then he excused her so he and I could talk.

He quickly apologized and asked, "What's so bad about this exception that it would bring you all the way to Texas?"

"Who is this client you would break policy for, and why?" I asked him.

"The client is Mr. Cisco, the ex-mayor of this city and currently Secretary of Housing and Urban Development. His wife is the president of the city council. I trust the colonel enough to grant him the exception. Look, Loyall, I'm sorry I failed to put this in the log, but I'm the one who made the exception. What's the big deal?"

Robert was getting a little loud, so I told him, "You need to calm down. First off, you are not allowed to make an exception to policies I have set. Second, although I have not confirmed this with the client, I believe your exception opened a door that has allowed the colonel to steal $500,000 from Mr. Cisco's account."

"Oh, shit!" Robert said as he fell back in his chair.

"Yeah … Look, as hard as it may be to believe, I'm reasonably sure it's true, or I wouldn't be here."

Then I went over the findings with Robert. He just sat there with an expression of disbelief on his face. But he knew my reputation, and he knew I was serious. Besides, he'd heard me tell stories of stranger things.

"I can't believe this," Robert said. "I sat in on a number of meetings between the colonel and Mr. and Mrs. Cisco when he was setting up the account. Did you know they were roommates in college?"

"No. But look, Robert, the problem I have right now is that I've been unsuccessful in my attempts to reach Mr. Cisco. If I keep calling, he might call the colonel to ask why I'm calling. I need your help to get in touch with him."

"It's not likely I can reach Mr. Cisco, but I reckon I can reach his wife," Robert said.

"Great."

He called Mrs. Cisco at her office, told the secretary who he was, dropped a few names, and said it was an emergency. It took a couple of tries, but we finally got her on the phone. She knew who Robert was and immediately asked him what the emergency was. He introduced me and said I would explain.

"The emergency is about the brokerage account you and Mr. Cisco have with us," I told her.

"I'm listening. This had better be good."

"Have you or your husband ever authorized a withdrawal from this account to the Jackson High School Reunion account at the Wells Fargo Bank?"

"Yes, once. A couple of years ago, we made a small donation. I think it was like $500."

"Is it possible that your husband made other donations to that account without your knowledge?"

"It's possible," she said, "but not likely. Now you need to get to the point before I hang up."

"Of course. I'm sorry, Mrs. Cisco."

"Please, call me Barbara. Now, what is the emergency?"

"Barbara, I believe your rep, Colonel Brown, forged a document that was used to withdraw close to $500,000 from your brokerage account into the Jackson High School Reunion account at the bank. It was done in small increments over a two-year period."

"Oh, my God! Are you sure?"

"I'm sure that the money went out of your brokerage account and into the account at the bank. What I'm not sure is whether your husband authorized the transfers. I've been trying to reach him to verify my suspicion, but I haven't been able to so far."

"I'm certain he didn't, but I'll speak to him tonight to make sure."

"Barbara," I added, "it's important that neither you nor your husband tips the colonel off about our suspicions before I can get into his office to collect further evidence."

"Don't worry, we won't," she assured me. "I'll call you as soon as I confirm this with my husband. Thank you for your call, and I will be in touch."

I gave her my phone number, and we hung up. Robert and I sat there in amazement for a moment. "A highly decorated colonel of the United States Air Force is a thief."

Then it hit Robert like a ton of bricks. He could be charged with "failure to supervise" because he had screwed up in the use of the signature-guarantee stamp. "How much trouble am I in because of the signature-guarantee stamp?"

"Don't worry," I said. "You won't lose your job or go to jail, but it will hurt a little."

I didn't hear back from Barbara until the next morning. She confirmed that Mr. Cisco had authorized none of those transactions. Now, it was time to formalize my case against the colonel. Mr. Cisco wasn't due back in town for a few days, so we set a time and date to meet, and I flew back to Minnesota to brief the president and the chairman. It turned out the chairman and the colonel had become good friends.

My team was busy running the numbers and making sure we had no unusual activity with any of the colonel's other clients. I revoked the firm's privilege to use the signature-guarantee stamp, and I had the stamp returned to the home office. Then I went over everything that had transpired so far with my team.

After a few days, I flew back for the meeting with Mr. and Mrs. Cisco. I was a little surprised when I walked into the room. I had brought Robert and my assistant, to take notes. There were about six people already sitting around a huge conference table. Mr. Cisco had brought his attorney, his accountant, and his assistant. Mrs. Cisco had brought her assistant.

After introductions, I took the floor to tell the story. I told them I believed the colonel had stolen $450,000 from their account and transferred it into another account for his personal use. Mr. Cisco wanted to see the proof, so I went over my documentation with them. Then he went on a twenty-minute rant. He was furious, cursing and shouting about how this could have happened. He said he and the colonel had been good friends and college roommates. He also mentioned someone he employed to go over his books and financial affairs.

Not realizing that person was in the room. I remarked that these withdrawals were quite apparent and not hidden, so whoever this accountant was, should be fired.

Mr. Cisco turned to one of the gentlemen in the room and said, "That might happen as soon as this meeting is over."

I told Mr. and Mrs. Cisco I needed their signature certifying that these withdrawals were not authorized. "I will be meeting with Colonel Brown later today, and I'll be going over my findings with him to give him the opportunity to tell his side of the story. Barring any new information, I'll most likely terminate him and shut his office down. After that, I'll be meeting with the Assistant U.S. Attorney General to have the FBI assigned to the case, and sometime after that, they'll arrest him. If it's okay with you, I will have Robert take over your accounts. It'll take me about a week, but I will make sure your money is returned to you, with interest."

Mr. Cisco asked me, "What do you get out of all this?"

"This is what I do. I get nothing extra except the satisfaction of knowing he won't be doing this to anyone else."

Between them, Mr. and Mrs. Cisco must have thanked me twenty times, not just for catching the problem and resolving it but for taking the time to fly down and meet them face-to-face.

Finally, it was time to meet with the colonel himself. Robert set up a meeting that the colonel assumed was his normal update, at least until he saw me sitting there. He shook my hand and asked if I would be in town long enough for us to have lunch. Salespeople are always smiling and selling, every moment of every day.

I got down to business quickly. Once I know someone is a thief, I have very little time for pleasantries. As you can guess, I jumped in with both feet.

"Colonel Brown, my being here is no coincidence. I have evidence that you made several unauthorized transfers from the account of your clients, Mr. and Mrs. Cisco, into a bank account at Wells Fargo in the name of the Jackson High School Reunion. Those transfers totaled $450,000."

"This must be some kind of mistake," he said. "Why would I steal money from my clients? And two of my closest friends? I'll get in touch with the Ciscos and clear this up right away."

"That won't be necessary. I've met with them already, and I have sworn affidavits from them acknowledging that they did not authorize these transfers."

"Are you accusing me of stealing this money? What makes you think *I* did it? If the money is genuinely missing, it must have been my secretary. She's the one who processed all of that type of paperwork."

"I explored that possibility," I said. "While she did process the forged documents, you gave them to her, filled out in your handwriting. Also, you and your wife are the only authorized signers on the bank account." I showed him copies of the bank documents. "I also have copies of the paperwork showing you and your wife withdrawing money from the High School Reunion account and depositing it right into your joint bank account. So, I don't believe your secretary had anything to do with this. Just so you know, I have an auditor going through the files in your office as we speak."

"You have no right to talk to my clients, go through my files, or look at my bank accounts! My attorney will have a field day suing you and this company. And as soon as I call the chairman, your ass will be out of a job so quick, it will make your head spin. You'll regret all these false accusations and straight-out lies. You'll never work in this field again. If this was the military, I would have your ass court-martialed!"

I was sure everyone in the office could hear him screaming by now.

"You're free to call whoever you like. The chairman is already aware of what's going on here, and there is absolutely no chance he will get involved. As far as my rights go, if you read over your contract that you signed, you'll find it gives me the right to do everything I've done. And more … You are hereby terminated. Robert will make arrangements for you to get your personal belongings. Is there anything you'd like to tell me, or any questions you have for me?"

"This isn't over, not by any means! You'll be hearing from my attorney as soon as possible."

I nodded. "I'm sure this is not over."

I always feel a responsibility to inform the staff and other reps in the office of what's going on as soon as it is appropriate, especially if they could hear all the commotion through the walls, anyway. Plus, you never know what kind of negative publicity might come out surrounding these types of situations, so the staff needs to be as prepared as possible. After the colonel left, I called a meeting of everyone in the office.

My last meeting of the day was at the Assistant U.S. Attorney General's office. As always, I had a nicely gift-wrapped investigation for them to go over. The FBI found the case particularly interesting because it involved a highly decorated colonel of the Air Force, the secretary of HUD, and the president of the city council.

As I told you, these situations often have a long tail on them. It took the FBI three months to arrest the colonel. This tail was so long that the colonel managed to get another job. Someone saw a newspaper article announcing the colonel's appointment as director of finance for the Houdon Corporation.

I showed our attorneys this and asked them if there was anything I could do. They said absolutely not. So, as the chief compliance officer of the company, I did nothing. But as a concerned private citizen, on plain white paper from my own home, and using a stamp I bought myself …

Apparently, the colonel lost his job that same week after the Houdon Corporation received an anonymous letter.

A couple of weeks later, the FBI finally got around to arresting him. I heard his wife arrived at the local office making threats, waving a gun around, and asking for me. I saw her at the hearing, but she wasn't as adamant about seeing me when she didn't have her gun.

It didn't stop there though. A year later, someone sent a tip into FINRA, complaining about me and the company I worked for. Because of the highly publicized events surrounding Bernie Madoff, FINRA were very sensitive about tips they received and so made it their business to follow them up aggressively.

They showed up at my office one day asking to do a surprise audit. From the information they requested and the questions they asked, I knew right away why they were there.

I told the inspector, "I know you won't answer me on this, but

I believe you're here based on a tip. I believe the tip came from an angry lady in Texas. I also believe that if you research this, you'll find she is angry because I fired her husband and had him put in jail for five years for stealing $450,000 from a client. It would save us both a lot of time and aggravation if you look at that first."

Well, he didn't answer me or acknowledge what I said was true. But the next day, they closed their investigation and canceled the audit.

I smile to myself when I think back on what the colonel said when I first met him. How he would serve his clients like he had served our country. Makes you wonder how he really served our country.

A Teaching Moment

Never get too busy to watch your own accounts. Trust but verify. If you're a busy person and traveling all the time, you need to hire someone on the outside to look at your accounts.

Don't just have a third party run the numbers to make sure they add up on both sides of the ledger. Give that person enough information to ask intelligent questions, like why was this withdrawal made? Where did the money go? Did the client authorize it? And if you see something unusual on your statement, don't just ask the rep. Seek a second opinion. The rep's answer might sound reasonable, but they might be hiding something.

CHAPTER 19

Mr. Scum Bag

A LADY CALLED in one day and said, "My friend, Jim Olson, passed away. Our granddaughter told me that he didn't have life insurance, but I know he did—Jim and I had the same insurance agent. I was hoping that someone there could help us."

"Okay. What's your name?" I asked.

"Dorothy Hubble."

"Good, thank you, Mrs. Hubble. So what is your relationship with Jim?"

"Jim and I lived together for forty years, though we were never married. Our children have passed away, but God blessed us with one beautiful granddaughter and she helps me with everything."

"Mrs. Hubble, is it possible for me to speak to your granddaughter?"

"She's at work. She can't talk until she gets off, and you'll be closed by then."

"Okay. I'll give you my cell number so she can call me at home."

"That would be great," Mrs. Hubble said. "My granddaughter's name is Helen."

Helen called that evening. She said she didn't know for sure but Mrs. Hubble was adamant that she and Jim had life insurance. They'd bought the insurance at the same time. Helen and Jim were the beneficiaries of Mrs. Hubble's policy, and Helen and Mrs. Hubble were the beneficiaries of Jim's policy. Both Helen and Mrs. Hubble hadn't been able to find any insurance policies. Helen had called the company and was told that the company had no policies for either Jim or Mrs. Hubble.

However, Jim and Mrs. Hubble both had premiums charged to their credit cards. I asked her who the agent was, and she told me his name was Levy Bag. I told Helen I'd do some research and call her back in a day or two.

The next morning, I researched all three names. All I found was that Mr. Bag had worked for us about fifteen years ago. We had no records at all for Jim or Mrs. Hubble.

I called Helen to ask if she had any documentation that might help. She sent me a copy of Mr. Bag's business card, some old letters from him, and some credit-card statements.

After reviewing these, I still found nothing proving they had life insurance with us. None of the letters were dated, and they were all low-quality photocopies on outdated letterheads. I had no way of knowing when those letters were sent; plus they made no direct mention of life insurance.

Even the credit-card statement only showed that the money was debited by the Levy Bag Company. In my heart, I felt something was wrong. But, of course, I could not go to the general counsel with only a feeling.

Helen told me that Mrs. Hubble and Jim had tons of old paperwork in their house, but she didn't know what to look for, and Mrs. Hubble was suffering from Alzheimer's. Mrs. Hubble told me Mr. Bag was the agent for several people in her complex, and she had heard of four other people who died and whose family said they didn't have life insurance when she knew Mr. Bag had sold them all insurance.

I flew out to Philadelphia to see what I could discover myself. The company's record only said Mr. Bag had voluntary resigned. It was the lack of information that concerned me. We have an in-house question that tells us if the person left on good terms or bad. The question is "Did they have cake or no cake?" and they told me he had no cake, meaning he left on bad terms.

Mrs. Hubble was living in a senior-citizen housing complex. She was a very nice lady, and I wanted to help her, but I felt uncomfortable being there alone with her. Helen was supposed to meet me there, but she was running late. Within the first hour, Mrs. Hubble had asked me three times who I was and why I was there.

I knew very little about Alzheimer's, just a few things I had read or seen on TV; I'd never come face-to-face with it.

The longer I spoke with Mrs. Hubble, the more daunting the situation became. I knew I wouldn't get a lot done without the help of her granddaughter.

I became especially concerned when I heard Mrs. Hubble call her granddaughter on the phone and tell her that some strange man was in her house going through her things and it scared her. Helen calmed her down and told her to put me on the phone. Thank God she was pulling into the parking lot as we spoke.

We went through tons of papers, but I found nothing useful. I asked about the other people who Mrs. Hubble thought had bought life insurance from Mr. Bag, but she said the ones she knew of had died and she didn't know how to reach their families. The only interesting thing we had was the credit-card statements showing that the money was being deducted for the Levy Bag Company. But it didn't say why.

For the first time in my career as a compliance officer, I felt helpless. I knew Mr. Bag had been taking advantage of people, but I didn't have a way to prove it. I needed more tangible evidence to connect him to insurance fraud and to a time frame when he was working for us. Without this connection, I wouldn't be able to convince the attorneys to go after him.

Helen and I spent a few more hours going through boxes of old papers but came up with nothing. It had grown quite late. I was tired, hungry, and needed to catch a plane in the morning, so I called it a night.

Once I returned to Minnesota, I continued to do as much research as I could but kept coming up with nothing but dead ends. Then two weeks later, I got a call from a senior-citizen's protection organization out of Philadelphia. They were investigating a credit-card fraud case against Mr. Levy Bag and wanted to speak with me. In fact, they were following up on a few complaints from other people in Mrs. Hubble's senior-citizen complex. They'd heard I was investigating Mr. Bag too and wanted to see if we could help each other. They were very interested in any information I was willing to share.

God has a way of working things out. I couldn't get Mr. Scum Bag on securities fraud, but they got him on credit-card fraud. Mr. Bag ended up going to jail for six years.

Someone once told me that, "a compliance officer was like being a Maytag repairman—it's a lonely job." Well, maybe but it's a very rewarding job.

CHAPTER 20

Cybersecurity

I AM ALWAYS thinking about how to protect clients, the firm, and the reps from themselves. But when it comes to cybersecurity threats, you don't know who the criminals are or where they are. All you can do is put together good policies and procedures to protect clients and hope the reps follow them.

Even the best policies and procedures won't protect the clients if no one follows them. It's not just the rep's or the company's responsibility, it's the client's too. Clients have to do their part to protect themselves. The firm spends millions of dollars to protect client data. But most clients with computers and emails may only spend $50–$100 to protect their own systems. Both the client and the firm have to do a better job. Here's why I say that.

An email request came into a rep's office asking for $25,000 to be wired to a bank account for some home improvements. From previous email conversations, the rep was aware the client was planning to do some home-improvement work, so the idea wasn't unfamiliar.

The problem was, the client's personal email had been hacked. But at the time, no one knew it. The email appeared to have come from the client, and the imposter was using buzzwords the actual client had used in the past. Plus, the rep knew the client had an account at the bank the money was being wired to.

Our procedures dictated that every email request for a withdrawal or transfer *must* be confirmed by a phone call. If the money was going to an account other than the client's own account, we also needed a written request that was signature guaranteed. The imposter seemed to be aware of our policies, and they said in the email they were traveling and wouldn't be available by phone. Plus, the contractor was waiting for the money, so they needed this done right away.

The rep's email reply stated they needed the request in writing and signed by the client. So, the imposter faxed a copy of a signed letter.

However, the letter needed to be signature guaranteed. To guarantee someone's signature, they must be physically present in front of you, which the client was not. Both the rep and her assistant wanted to expedite the process to please the client, so the rep retrieved the faxed letter, and the assistant stamped it with our signature-guarantee stamp. Then the assistant sent the request to the home office to be processed. The cover sheet for the request asked if it had been confirmed by a phone call; someone marked "yes" in the box. The cover sheet also asked if the signature had been guaranteed in the office. Someone marked the box, "yes."

Back at the branch office, the rep had received three emails asking if the transfer had been made. The home office, having documents stating that all the requirements had been met, wired the money out. When a wire transfer is made, the home office sends an email to the rep and the client, as well as a confirmation letter to the client's home address.

The next morning, having been informed by the rep that the first wire transfer went through, the imposter, sent another email request saying the contractor had run into a problem. The project would cost twice as much, and to please send another $50,000 with the same instructions. When the home office received this second request, they felt it was unusual for this client and called the rep to ask if they had spoken with the client to confirm it. The rep said she had, indeed, confirmed the request. By then, the rep had received two emails from the imposter asking if the transfer had been completed.

The rep told the imposter, by email, that it might speed things up if they call the home office themselves. This was actually against our policy because only the rep knows the client's voice. But the imposter did just that. They were smart enough to know that the home office wouldn't know their voice, and they had gathered enough information from the real client's email to answer any security questions the home office might ask. With that, the second transfer was completed.

The home-office person processing these requests still felt uncomfortable about this new activity in the client's account. Their review had shown that the client had never requested a transfer before and was now suddenly making two back-to-back requests.

The home-office processor tried to call the client using the phone number in the files. That number was no longer valid, so they called the rep to get the client's number. They were unable to reach the client until late that evening, but as soon as they did, the real client confirmed their suspicions and said he had never requested a wire transfer.

Kudos to the home-office person for following his gut.

The client acknowledged he had spoken to the rep in general conversation about one day having some work done on the house. But he said he hadn't spoken to the rep in months, by either phone or email. It was clear that the rep had not followed procedures at all.

That's when I got a call at home. I told the home-office person to put everything on my desk and I would take it from there.

First thing in the morning, I called the bank. Most companies, especially banks, are traditionally very hesitant to give out any information about a client, no matter the circumstances. I spoke to the people in the bank's fraud unit, but they would not tell me anything. I kind of expected that, but at least I could put them on notice that something was wrong in the hope they would put a hold of some sort on the account. Because of the U.S. Patriot Act and changes to the Bank Secrecy Act, however, some financial institutions have formed agreements to share information with other financial institutions. They eventually told me that the money had been withdrawn.

My next call was to the client. I explained the sequence of events and told him I believed his personal email had been hacked and the imposter had acquired a lot of the client's personal information. The client was upset about the breakdown in procedures but was somewhat understanding about how it could happen. I assured him that every dollar would be replaced in his account as if nothing had happened, and I promised him I would get to the source of the breakdown and take appropriate action. All I needed from him was a signed affidavit of forgery, and I would take care of everything.

As it turned out, this branch was local and only an hour's drive from the home office. To make it more interesting, though, the rep involved was the daughter of the managing partner. I first placed a call to the office to make sure they were there. When I walked into the office, the whole room went quiet. I had known Jeff, the managing partner, for more than fifteen years, but never had a reason to go to his office. He knew when he saw me that it wasn't going to be a good day.

I had brought an assistant with me and had her start an audit of some files while I spoke with Jeff. The first thing he said was, "I know you don't do social visits, so what is this all about?"

"Let's go into your office," I suggested.

Once we were inside, I continued, "I have a serious problem that involves Sonja, your office manager, and Monica, your daughter. They both failed to follow policy and procedures, and so someone was able to withdraw $75,000 from a client's account."

Then I explained the entire sequence of events. He asked me how serious it was. I told him, "Short of any new information, this is what's going to happen. I will interview both of them today to hear their side of the story. As a courtesy, if you want to keep this out of the public eye and not have everyone in your office looking in on us, I would be willing to meet them at my office."

"I'd appreciate that very much."

"I believe that both Monica and Sonja deliberately ignored the policies and procedures for wire transfers. As a result, a client was harmed and $75,000 was taken out of his account. Because of the magnitude of the event, it must be reported to FINRA, who will hold their own hearing and investigation and possibly take additional action against both of them. FINRA will then turn their focus on you for failure to supervise. So I will be taking serious action against both of them: Sonja has been reprimanded in the past for not following procedures for the use of the signature-guarantee stamp, so she'll have to be terminated. With Monica, it will depend on her statement, but at a minimum, she'll be fined and suspended for a period of time. But I can't rule out she also might have to be terminated.

"Then there is the question of who will pay the money back. If your firm pays, it could go a long way in deciding what happens to Monica. If not, I will go after Monica herself for the money."

I saw the tears in his eyes had started to roll down his face. His biggest goal in life had been to build his dream business and leave it to his only daughter to run after his retirement.

"When FINRA reviews my report, they'll decide whether I took appropriate action. If they feel that I didn't do enough, they'll take additional action against her. I have no idea when or what that might be."

Jeff spoke to both Monica and Sonja after I left. He had them put their statements in writing to bring to the meetings at my office. No new information emerged from the interviews or their statements, though, so things progressed quickly.

After I closed out my investigation, here's what happened. Sonja, the office manager, admitted she had guaranteed the client's signature without ever seeing the client and that she falsely marked the form to say that all the steps were followed. She told me she had guaranteed the signature because the client had faxed in a copy of his driver's license, and she had compared the signatures. But our policies did not allow for that, and to make matters worse, if she had actually looked at the faxed copy of the driver's license, she would have seen it had expired two years ago. Because Sonja had already been reprimanded for misuse of the signature-guarantee stamp, she was terminated.

Monica, the registered rep, admitted that she hadn't followed procedure by confirming the order by phone. She was suspended for three months without pay, fined $5,000 and required to take some continuing education classes. Also, she was required to pay the $75,000 back to the client, which her father agreed to pay on her behalf.

Jeff, because he was her supervisor and because further investigation showed that he had signed off on the orders without inquiring as to the validity, was fined $3,000 and required to take additional continuing education classes.

The client was paid back all his money plus interest. The perpetrator was never discovered, but the information was turned over to the FBI.

Remember when I said that these things often have long tails? Well, two years after these events, FINRA decided to take additional action against Monica. They suspended her from the business for an additional six months and fined her another $10,000.

A TEACHING MOMENT

Cybercriminals are very patient and are almost impossible to catch. They can hack into your personal email without you knowing, gathering information, and possibly waiting years until the right time comes to use it.

BACK TO THE STORY

Remember the faxed copy of the driver's license which had been expired for two years? That told me the real client had sent his driver's license somewhere via email at one time or another.

The imposter must have hacked into the client's email two years earlier and been sitting on that information, waiting for the right opportunity to use it.

People must periodically change their passwords. Be careful what information you put in emails. If you do business by email, check your email daily and check your accounts often to look for anything suspicious. For registered reps, don't cut corners. The policies and procedures are there to protect you and your clients, not to take business away from you.

Take the time to smell the roses. Don't be in such a hurry that you overlook something unusual. Look for red flags, and if you find something, suspicious, say something. If your clients say "Don't call me" in an email, that's a red flag. If a client asks you via email to do something they've never requested before, that's a red flag. It's better to be safe than sorry. Your client will thank you later.

This story hit close to home because something similar happened to me. I received an email one day from my brother, Rennie—or I thought it was from my brother. He told me he was in Philadelphia visiting some friends when he had a seizure. He said he was in the hospital and asked if I could send him some money. Rennie was prone to seizures, so it wasn't an unusual situation. I emailed him back and said of course, how much do you need? He told me a $1,000 and to send it in the name of his friend, who would pick the money up for him. Red flag.

I called my mom and asked if she'd heard from Rennie. She told me he was in the backyard cutting the grass. She called him to the phone, and I told him what happened.

"So were you going to send the money?" he asked.

"Yeah, of course."

"Great. How about you send it anyway?"

"F*** you, bro!" I laughed and hung up.

I emailed the imposter back, told him I had sent the money, and gave him a fake confirmation number. I smiled at the thought that he would have to drive to the Western Union office in heavy traffic and stand in line only to find that no money had been sent and the number he had was wrong. Hopefully, he'd at least be caught on camera, and that might one day be used against him. Who knows? Anyway, I never heard back from him.

CHAPTER 21

Forgery Is Against the Law

THE CRIME OF forgery generally involves making a fake document, changing the existing one, or supplying a signature without authorization. Forgery also involves a false document signature, used with the intent to deceive.

I already said confession is good for the soul. So, before I tell you this story, here's a little confession about the first and only time I was ever involved personally in forgery.

When I was in elementary school, on the last report card before summer vacation one year, I had four "A"s, three "B"s, and one "E"— that was before they started using "F"s. I knew my mother was going to "beat the black off me" for getting that "E." So, I changed the "E" to a "B." I figured that school was out, and my mother worked two jobs, so she wouldn't have time to go check it out.

The problem was the letter "E" was written in red ink. She must have wondered why I got a red "B." Well, I learned two lessons that day: one, never think you're smarter than your mother; two, the consequences for forgery can be very painful. She may not have actually beat the black off me, but my skin was so red from the belt lashes, you would have thought she had.

Over the following years, I found so many cases of reps signing for clients. I actually interviewed fifty reps, and almost every one of them admitted they thought it was ok to do so. For example, if a client forgot to sign one page of an application, the rep would just sign it for them.

I couldn't fire everyone if this had been an acceptable practice at the firm. So I put out a memo saying that from now on, signing for a client was unacceptable with or without their permission, and reminding everyone that forgery was against the law. I then had every rep in the company sign an acknowledgment that they read and understood this.

It was much too difficult to determine whether someone was forging a client's signature as an accommodation when a client forgot or because they were hiding something from the client. So to make life easier and to remove the guesswork, I banned it for any reason. We had also lost a large lawsuit in which a client lost thousands of dollars in an investment and passed away, and her daughter sued us, saying that her mother, the client, had never signed for the investment. She pointed to the signature on the application as evidence, and it was obvious that someone else had signed it.

I couldn't have reps signing applications for investments the clients never knew they had, just to make more commissions. And I couldn't sit around making judgment calls whether there was ill intent or not. So, my policy was: if you sign a client's signature, you will be terminated.

Anyway, an application came in one day for a high-risk investment for an elderly client. I called the client to verify that she understood the risk and truly wanted to buy this product. She told me that she recalled the rep talking to her about it but never gave her permission to buy it, let alone to sign on her behalf.

This rep was the son of our largest managing partner so I needed to make sure I had all my ducks in a row. Before I called the rep, for instance, I had to make sure it wasn't his assistant who forged the document.

The assistant told me she remembered the application because it was such a large investment. She told me that the rep had needed to get the order in to qualify for a trip. He had told her the client wasn't available and would sign it later, so the assistant sent the application in for processing, only for it to be rejected because there was no signature. She returned it to the rep, saying he needed the client's signature. The rep returned the application to the assistant fifteen minutes later with a signature. She didn't question it, just sent it in for processing. She knew that the rep never left the office though.

Once I had that information, I called the rep in for questioning. After I laid out all the evidence in front of him, he acknowledged he had forged the application. His excuse was that the client would have signed it but was unavailable and he needed to get it in right away.

I knew all eyes would be on me on this one. Some people thought he was too big a rep to be fired over one incident. But my policy left no room for exceptions. I told him that if he had called me in advance and I had verified it with the client, I would have accepted the trade so he could qualify for the trip. But he made the wrong decision and must suffer the consequences.

I terminated him on the spot. He threw a fit for about a half hour before he left. He also held true to his threat of getting an attorney and suing me. I'm not sure why reps think they can sue me personally and that the company wouldn't back me up with a roomful of attorneys. But they do, and they always lose … as he did.

CHAPTER 22

Retirement Day

THE CARDS AND letters were once again rolling in. This time, they were congratulating me on twenty years of service. Everywhere I went, people were stopping to shake my hand to thank me for all I had done. After twenty years of putting out financial fires, it was time to call it a day. My retirement day.

I had made a difference, and I'm not just talking about the numbers, but people's lives and their hearts. Compliance was no longer the ugly stepchild, no longer considered a necessary evil. It was now at the forefront of everyone's mind. If I left a legacy it was to say "no" when appropriate and always do the right thing.

At my retirement party, the home office presented me with the Legion award to show their appreciation for all I had done.

Who knew that saying "no" could make such a difference?

I thank my boss for having my back and giving me the keys to the car. I thank my team for trusting me and standing strong and believing we were making a difference.

Most of all, I thank God for kicking my chair.

I would like to leave you with this poem:

The designer of life has provided the means
To do what it would take to fulfill all my dreams
He has given me obstacles to make me see
That some things must be worked for

And won't necessarily come free
He has given me the choice to have sight or be blind
To be constructive with life or destructive with time
He has given me the gift of knowledge to share
And the strength to carry burdens I bear
So, with all this ability it's truly up to me
To be the designer of my life
As He sees fit for it to be.

CPSIA information can be obtained
at www.ICGtesting.com
Printed in the USA
FFHW020740080219
50478300-55701FF